Homeless in America:

The Solution

by

Jeremy Reynalds

Huntington House Publishers

Huntington House Publishers
P.O. Box 53788
Lafayette, Louisiana 70505

Library of Congress Card Catalog Number 93-80788
ISBN 1-56384-063-4

Contents

Introduction

What you're about to read has been culled from years of living through spiritual hard knocks and the Lord's Institute of Life-Long Learning.

When I commenced my ministry to the homeless, I had "ministry" on my mind-you know, spiritual stuff. I had no idea that that included formulating budgets, keeping neighbors happy, dealing with county fire, health, and zoning departments. But it does. It all goes with the territory. Oh, and then there's dancing with the IRS, and establishing non-profit corporations, and receiving and maintaining federal tax exemption status!

This book has a specific purpose: to encourage you to obey God's calling if He's leading you to be involved in full-time ministry. It's also designed to help you "do it right," avoiding bringing any reproach upon yourself or the body of Christ locally or nationally. Ministry is not glamorous–and it's not easy–but, if you're doing it to obey God's call upon your life it's the most rewarding thing you can ever do. If you want to be in full-time ministry for any other reason than to obey God's call, don't. If God has called you to full-time ministry, then dive right in, but be aware what you're getting into by reading this book very carefully. Feel free to contact me if I can help you.

This book is dedicated to the Lord, without whom none of this would have ever happened; my long-suffering, dedicated, and wonderful wife Sylvia; and my five children, Ben, Joshua, Jeremiah, Joel, and Josiah. It is also dedicated to Gino Geraci, pastor of Calvary Chapel of South Denver; Carl Conley; Frank Tercero, a great friend for over a decade and the best business manager and operations manager a shelter could ever want; Pastor Gary Cowan of Harvest Chapel; Pastor Bernie Frazier of New Life Fellowship, and Pastor Pete Bradford, an inner city missionary in Los Angeles and a great friend for over a decade as well. Thanks also go to Carol Cook, for the help and the friendship, and University of New Mexico professors Fred Bales and Hank Trewhitt. Thanks to Blackie Gonzales of KDAZ Radio and KCHF TV 11. Last but not least, thanks also to a great secretary, Dotty Dooley, and to everyone who's helped me so much over the years, but whom I've left out.

For more information, I can be contacted by mail at P.O. Box 27693, Albuquerque, New Mexico 87125; by telephone at (505) 877-6967; and by fax at (505) 873-2708.

Chapter One

My Story: Growing Up in England

I lay in bed and listened to the muffled, angry voices coming from the living room. My heart began to pound. Mom and dad were arguing again. What about I didn't know; I just knew they were arguing.

At eleven years old, I hated my parents' almost nightly fights. I knew my mother wasn't happy living with my wheelchair-bound father, diagnosed several years earlier with multiple sclerosis. On a number of occasions, she had told me that if dad hadn't been sick, she would have left him. On other occasions, mom informed me that I should be grateful she stuck around to take care of my older brother and me. Lots of parents wouldn't have done the same, she added. Mom explained to me that she only married my father because he had told her that he would apply for a commissioned officer's position in Britain's Royal Air Force. He didn't apply, and now, in light of his disability, there was no chance of that. She felt cheated and angry.

As sharp tones filtered through the muffled voices, I focused on the one bright spot on the horizon–I would be leaving for boarding school in a few weeks. That which I initially looked forward to as an escape from family tensions, however, became my own private nightmare. Nights brought on being the victim of schoolboy pranks, like having my bed shortsheeted. Days were filled with planning escapes from hockey games, rugby football, cricket or cross-country running—depending on the semester. I didn't seem to fit in anywhere, so I retreated into a world of books, where no one demanded anything from me.

The school was in Bournemouth, only about an hour's bus ride from my home on England's south coast. Ironically, my escape was to go home many weekends—to the home I had been trying so hard to escape from. I guess I concluded that the tension at home was preferable to the abject misery I endured at school.

There were a few fun times. One early morning, all the kids in my dorm awoke at about two o'clock, buzzing with excitement. The chapel was on fire. Since a burned down chapel meant no chapel services in the morning, and maybe for a long time, the kids were elated. In my state of reprobation, these chapel services were extremely boring—just something else in my life to be endured.

Of course, the next morning, the fire and how it was discovered was the talk of the campus, and did we love what we found out! The word was that the school chaplain had gone to a dance in a nearby town. Returning in the early hours of the morning, he found the chapel on fire. However, this "hip" spiritual advisor hadn't gone to the dance dressed in robe and cassock. No sir, he was in full sixties regalia, including a Beatles-style wig and high-heeled boots. Naturally, we all thought this was hilarious. No one talked of anything else for days after.

Christian Things

The last few math lessons of each semester were "different." Our math teacher was a born-again Christian. For a "treat" at the end of each semester, the teacher asked us if we would like him to read to us. Naturally we agreed, even though his choice of books wasn't ours. (But then, anything beat math!) The teacher's readings-of-choice were evangelical Christian books, usually dramatic life-stories about a hero of the faith who had done wonderful things for the Lord. While I didn't agree with the Lord of the books, the stories were very gripping and easily held my attention.

I took it upon myself to argue with this teacher about Christianity's irrelevance to the culture. Since I was also going through a non-meat-eating period—I mean, I was really into it—in one of the many discussions I had with this instructor, I told him that Jesus was a vegetarian. He responded that what was more important than what Jesus ate was what He had done for me on the cross. I also informed my long-suffering instructor that Christianity was a crutch for the intellectually feeble and old women. Still, those end-of-term stories stayed with me.

I wanted to study sociology, and the boarding school didn't offer anything like it, so I finished my last couple of years of school back in Bournemouth, living at home again. I still didn't fit in any better; it was a different school, with different people, but I encountered the same misery—desperately lonely and feeling like an outsider.

I threw myself into my new-found studies of sociology and English literature and soon adopted all the latest sociological buzz-words into my vocabulary. You know, stuff like Karl Marx's "Religion is the opiate of the people."

I remember scoffing at various religious posters I saw plastered around Bournemouth. I proudly declared, "I'm not a Christian. I'm an agnostic. You can't tell if there's a God." My mother was bitterly angry about this, but I reasoned that if the Bible is not true—and I had already made up my mind that it wasn't—then Christianity's false since the Bible is the basis for the religion.

Desperate for friends, I eagerly welcomed attention of any type. I was sitting in the student lounge one day when an attractive young lady came up to me and just started talking. I soon learned that her name was Jenny Griffith. There was a "hook" to the conversation. Jenny invited me to church. I didn't relish the prospect, but I definitely liked the idea of seeing more of Jenny, so I went. I was in for a shock. This wasn't anything I had imagined. My idea of church was based on very formal, proper, incense-burning Anglican parishes.

This church wasn't like that at all. It was very small, and it had no organ. There were seats and not pews. The congregation sang lively, up-tempo songs and sounded as if they enjoyed being there. Everyone was very friendly. I liked it. This was definitely unlike any other type of church or religious experience I had encountered before.

I continued to go back to this small, friendly, informal little church–although not for the right reasons. I was hoping there might be the possibility of a relationship springing up between Jenny and myself. The Lord, meanwhile, had other things in mind–like my salvation!

The Gospel Hits Home

Following one Sunday night service, the pastor approached me and asked me if I wanted to do anything about "it." I asked him what "it" was, and he again responded by saying "it." I told him not right now, and that was the end of the conversation.

It wasn't until much later that I learned that Pastor Phillip Powell was really asking me if I wanted to commit my life to Jesus Christ. He didn't want to be overly pushy and force the situation, as I was the first visitor to the church for a long time, hence the mystery. They didn't want me to run out the door and never come back again.

As the weeks went on, I continued to attend church. Curiously, I even started listening to contemporary Christian music at home. And I was also developing an interest in what the pastor was saying. The Lord's hook had caught another fish, and it was time to reel it in. While not initially attending Jenny's church to hear about Jesus, I heard the Word preached and taught, and now it was beginning to take effect.

One day, I purchased a copy of a modern translation of the Bible, *Good News for Modern Man*, and for the first time I read that Bible with an open mind, not considering myself to be intellectually superior. I picked up the Bible for the first time and said, "God, if you're real, please speak to me in a way I can understand." At that point, I had some sort of a supernatural experience. The letters on the Bible page in front of me appeared to be about six feet high. From that point on, I knew the Bible was true. I had asked God to intervene in my life in a way I could understand, and He honored my request. It was very biblical. The Word says if you seek Him, you shall find Him. That supernatural experience was over sixteen years ago—a one-of-a-kind experience. There's never been anything like it since.

Now, despite that experience, I still wasn't saved. I hadn't trusted Jesus. The Lord was just supernaturally preparing my heart to do so. I didn't know how to get saved. A week later I was reading a book by an Anglican clergyman named David Watson. He made a very simple statement to the effect that if you have never asked Jesus Christ to be your Lord and Savior, then you are not a Christian, and you will be eternally lost.

My newfound belief in the Bible swept away any reasons to hesitate. I bowed my head and asked Jesus Christ to be the Lord of my life. There were no flashing lights and no more supernatural experiences, just a quiet act of obedience to God's Word. At that point, the future course and direction of my life was set. I was a Christian, and God was getting ready to do some exciting things both in me and for me. My mother began to get rather worried about my sudden religious fanaticism. At first she wasn't too worried; she thought I would get over it. Then as my faith began to increase rather than dissipate, she became very concerned. My mother even went so far as to make an appointment for me with a local parish priest. But by the time I left the reverend's office, I think he had given up on me. He asked me if I really thought that anyone who didn't receive Jesus Christ as his Lord and Savior would go to hell. Assuring him that I most definitely believed just that, he terminated the interview, sadly shaking his head.

Bible School

I felt the need to receive some Bible college instruction, so I spent the 1976–1977 academic year at a Bible college in South Wales. It was a good experience—like being in a spiritual hothouse. I can still remember some of what my lecturers said. There was the assistant principal of the school, who had as one of his favorite sayings: "People want to work to become Christians, but after they become Christians, they don't want to work." Oh, how true!

Of course, if I had paid as much attention to my Greek instructor as I did to other aspects of Bible college life, I might have ended up learning some Greek. Unfortunately, while the instructor was trying to instruct us in all the basics, I was goofing off. Consequently, Greek is still "Greek" to me to this day.

After my year at Bible College, I returned home to Bournemouth, where the burning question became what I planned to do with my life. I also began to feel that God might be calling me to full-time ministry. This was a fascinating challenge for me at the time. The church in England in which I was saved didn't give young people the opportunity of a decision about obeying God's calling in their life. In other words, you couldn't decide individually to obey God; someone had to decide for you. Still, I followed the call, so I applied to a couple of universities and also to London Bible College. I was accepted at LBC. However, shortly after being accepted by LBC, I began to sense God speaking to me about going to America. I applied then to Southeastern College in Lakeland, Florida, and was initially accepted. But that was only the beginning. There were still lots of other things to be worked out—such as how I planned to pay for everything.

While England is very generous in student financial aid, that generosity only extends to those attending British universities and colleges. They just weren't willing to finance a British student wanting to go to school in the United States. I was at a standstill—now unemployed, and with an acceptance at an American college only good if I could come up with the funds to make it a reality.

Meanwhile, things were a little rocky at church youth group meetings, where I became the object of humor—especially when there were guest speakers. When everyone introduced themselves to guests and said what they did for a living, the kids started to preempt me. "Oh, that's Jeremy Reynalds, and he's going to America," they'd say.

The months continued to slip by, and I wasn't any closer to America. Had I missed God? Maybe I should give up the whole idea.

Then something very interesting happened. A few weeks later, I took the train from Bournemouth to London. I was going to meet with a man I'd been talking to on and off that year. I told him all my woes, hoping he might offer me some money. He didn't; instead, he told me, "Jeremy, you say that God has called you to America. But right now you've got a lot of time on your hands. I wish I had the amount of time you do. Go home and make up your mind that you're going. If you say that God has told you, then act on it."

While I was initially disappointed that David didn't give me any money, his advice started to cause a change in my thinking. God used this man's words to speak to my heart. I then knew that I'd be going to America.

America Here I Come!

Three days later, a lady who didn't profess any relationship with Christ asked me how things were going, then gave me two hundred dollars for the airfare. Ten days later, I was offered a place to stay in Orlando, Florida. It was from an English pastor and his wife, who opened their home to me without even knowing who I was.

Seventeen days later, I was on the plane. Even though I was there, physically flying across the Atlantic, it was still hard for me to do it. I had dreamed, hoped, and prayed for so long. Now my dream was becoming reality; although, maybe I wouldn't be here now if I had known everything that lay in store for me. It was time for me to grow up. I was on my own now.

For the last twenty years, I'd been relatively pampered. I'd been to private school and, even though I didn't care for it, had been guaranteed a roof over my head and three meals a day. I could have gone home to live and have been automatically assured of the same. Whether I worked or didn't really made no difference. Now it was just me and the Lord, and I'd have to take care of myself. My mother made it very clear to me that I was making my bed, and I would have to lie in it—face all the consequences. There wasn't going to be any help from her at all. She said she'd helped me enough, and now, she said, I was despising all her help—throwing my life away, and going to the "Colonies" on a wild goose chase, all because of that "fanatical religion."

She did have some excuse for the way she felt. My mother had taken wonderful care of both myself and my brother. We had both enjoyed English public school educations. (Don't get confused. A "public" school education in England means a "private" school in the U.S.) She felt she had done enough for us, and I admit I'd been less than gracious or wise in my comments since my salvation.

One morning, my mother and I were well into a big argument. I made the mistake of telling this good, upright, caring English woman that she was both a heathen and a sinner—technically true, but both unkind and unwise. To my mother, a sinner was someone like a prostitute, and a heathen was someone running around a jungle in Africa. My newfound Christian zeal needed some refining!

Some of the experiences that lay ahead of this young believer, I can see in retrospect, were the Lord's way of preparing me for my lifelong work of ministering to the poor and needy.

After an uneventful transatlantic flight, I arrived at Miami International Airport, clutching a one-way ticket to America along with fifty dollars remaining from the gift. In 1978, an Air Florida ticket from Miami to Orlando only cost twenty dollars. I was in America with thirty dollars in my pocket—all my worldly wealth.

I disembarked from the plane and made my way to Immigration. There were numerous booths from which I could choose, so I prayed, made my selection, and "marched boldly on." The official asked me what I planned to do while I was in the United States and how long I wanted to stay. When I told him I wanted to preach, he looked a little concerned and asked me, "Oh, you're not going to make a living at it, are you? There are people who make a lot of money doing that."

I assured him that I wouldn't make a lot (and after fifteen-and-a-half years, I can still say that's the case). Many years later I realized how the Lord went before me during that experience. I've been told that the immigration officer should have asked me if I had a return air ticket to England. If I couldn't produce one, he should have asked me if I had enough money to purchase one. But he didn't.

It looks to me like the Lord was serious about taking a little, middle-class English boy who had absolutely no personal experience of being poor, hungry, and homeless and sending him to the United States to help care for America's needy.

Finally, I arrived at the pastor's house in Orlando. A lady answered the door, introduced herself as Kathy, the pastor's wife, and said her husband would be back shortly. She gave me tea. (Naturally, we were English.) When her husband arrived, David and Kathy questioned me closely about my plans, and then made a statement which I still remember as clearly today as the day it was spoken: "Our faith has gotten us here, and if you want to get anywhere, it's going to have to be your faith that does it. You're not going to sponge off us, OK?"

I gulped a quick response. I mean, what else was I going to say? I was now in a foreign country, staying with strangers, and the immigration law prevented me from working while holding a visitors visa. I had nothing (sort of like the homeless people I would be helping years down the road–totally dependent on others for my needs).

Dave and Kathy's stated position wasn't quite what I had expected. All sorts of things went flooding through my mind the next few minutes. Maybe I could go back to England without losing too much face and reapply to London Bible College. Maybe . . . maybe . . . maybe . . . I was still trying to determine what I had really gotten myself into when the couple said they were really tired, showed me my room, and went to bed.

I lay in bed for a long time that night, thinking and wondering. It was obvious–and right–that this couple wasn't going to support me just because I said God had called me to America. They were letting me know that if God had really called me, they'd like to see some proof. I could see it coming, for them to say "You say God's called you to America. Well, He's called us as well. You're in our house, which is a tangible example of God providing for us. It has a pool and orange trees, and we have plenty of food in our pantry. If God *has* called you, He'll provide for you as well."

I was getting more scared by the minute. It's one thing to tell some kids in England that God has called you to another country. It sounds sort of grand, even if they don't believe you. And while I was telling those kids, I was still being provided for by my parents.

Now God would have to be my provider, or I'd starve, or be deported in great embarrassment.

A couple of days passed, including my first visit to an American church. While I didn't know it, and can't even remember seeing her, sitting in that service was someone who would make a great difference in my life–my future wife. But the "big event" I remember from that first service wasn't the sermon or the church building. It was seeing that the church had a secretary. This was my first evidence of culture shock manifesting itself to me. All the evangelical churches I'd visited while in England had been small and poor. In one, the church didn't even have an office for the pastor; he worked out of his house.

A Different Side of the U.S.A.

A day or two later, Dave and Kathy came up with what they thought was a brilliant idea to introduce me first hand to the realities of American life. They "suggested"–and with my financial situation, who was I to refuse–that I should spend the summer with a bunch of pentecostal holy rollers who travelled the U.S. holding tent revivals.

So I loaded up a suitcase and met with a group of other young Christians from the Orlando area who were planning to spend their summer in the same way. We arrived in Anderson, South Carolina, at about one o'clock in the morning.

Everyone was asleep in pup-tents. Someone was kind enough to share his with me. Boy, did God have a sense of humor.

This was my introduction to a brand new way of living. We had long Bible studies in the morning and ate peanut butter and jelly for our lunches, or whatever was available. (As a result, to this day I still can't stand peanut butter.) In the afternoon, most of us went street-witnessing. Following that, we returned to camp, took showers, had an hour or so's free time, and then participated in a long evening revival service. Sometimes these evening services lasted into the three-hour range. Supper was *after* the evening service.

Again, in retrospect, I see how the Lord was molding me for my life's work. While in England, I truly never knew what it was like to be poor. I had everything I physically needed, and as I said earlier, despite not enjoying my experience in the English private school system, it is still an experience that is sought after and envied by many.

England has (or had when I was there) what is known as council housing. Here in the U.S., the equivalent would be project housing. Now back in the sixties and seventies, the majority of this housing was painted a dull, drab uniform grey color. My image of poor people, their needs, hopes, and problems, was shaped by listening to my mother make derogatory comments about the occupants of the so-called council houses, who had apparently ended up in project-style housing because of some inner deficiency. She believed, as many did, that they could have something better if they really wanted.

You can see that the Lord had to lead me gradually into His chosen calling for my life. Talk about a strange election. I really can't think of any more unlikely person to minister to the needs of the poor than myself. My background was prejudiced against it.

The Lord did many wonderful things for me my first summer in the United States, in particular giving me many opportunities to share His Word. Many of these were quite humorous. Pat, the evangelist in charge of the young folks that first summer, was constantly being asked by a visitor to have me preach. After honoring the request a few times, Pat told the lady, "You must sure like what Jeremy has to say."

"Oh no," the lady responded, "I don't understand a word. It's just the way he says it!"

The Lord also showed me the wonders of His provision. He supplied my personal needs, as well as those of the whole group. Meals were provided by local church people who attended the meetings.

At the end of the summer, I returned to Orlando and was invited by Dave and Kathy to stay with them. Plans for attending the Bible college in Lakeland didn't work out, and I really didn't know what I was going to do. A few weeks after returning to Orlando, I met Sylvia, my future wife. We started dating in September 1978–a rather traumatic experience.

I didn't have any money, so we didn't really go out on dates; it was more of a "hanging-out" situation. I was also still very immature. Sylvia already had one child. At the time, she was working full-time in a daycare and had been on her own, supporting herself for years. I was scarcely on my own and didn't have any idea how to support myself, let alone a wife and a family.

A few months later, we got married; it was 14 April 1979. Sylvia paid for everything because I still couldn't work. She even bought the rings. We honeymooned in Bradenton, Florida, where we spent half the time by ourselves and the last three days with Ben, Sylvia's six-year-old son.

I was still chomping at the bit to be in full-time ministry but failed to see the Lord's guidance in a couple of things. I was looking at my life through my eyes instead of the Lord's, who took into consideration the significant step I had taken by getting married. I had also neglected to consider that there can be a significant time lag between receiving the call of God into ministry and actually going into action. The biblical example I have used many times to illustrate this is when the psalmist David was called to be king. Although the prophet anointed him, it wasn't until some time after that he actually took on the role of king. The waiting time didn't invalidate God's calling. It's just God's way of doing things.

Someone who is in tune with what the Holy Spirit is saying to them stores that word–that call–in their heart and knows they have something special set aside for them to perform in the future. Unfortunately, I wasn't in tune with God and wanted to be "God's little helper." I thought I could help God out by *not* waiting for His timing, consequently causing tremendous grief for my wife, family, and everyone around me.

I got a variety of things accomplished after we got married. Of course, one of the first was to apply for my "green card." If successful, that meant I could now be a registered alien, able to live and work (yes, work) permanently in the United States.

We filled out all the necessary reams of paperwork and were eventually summoned to a meeting with the Immigration and Naturalization Service in Tampa, Florida. I guess one of the major reasons for this meeting was to see if this was a legitimate request for a green card. Some aliens have gotten married (and then divorced) for the sole reason of staying in the country.

Fortunately, Sylvia was very pregnant by this time with the soon-to-be Joshua, so it was (I hope) obvious that I didn't intend to divorce her. Then the INS officer asked her my full name, and she couldn't remember. Still, he must have believed us because my request for permanent alien status was granted. For a few years after that, aliens had to register yearly through a card obtainable at the post office. Sylvia used to get a kick out of that because she'd go and ask for the registration card "for my alien husband."

Well, now I could work. The only problem was, I wasn't trained to do anything in particular. I worked a variety of spot jobs and attended some community college courses, all the time wanting to be in full-time ministry.

I just wouldn't wait, either.

Very foolishly, I launched myself into an extended volunteer ministry position. This resulted in our whole family becoming homeless in late 1981 and early 1982. A family in Central Florida very kindly agreed to shelter Sylvia and our two-and-a-half-year-old son Joshua, but because of my rotten attitude that kind offer didn't extend to me.

On the Road

With my wife and family sheltered, I set out on the road. I had enough money for a bus ticket to Dallas, and from then on, my mode of transportation was hitch-hiking. On a late evening in January 1982, it was cold in Dallas. I had about ten dollars in my pocket and a small suitcase, which seemed unbearably heavy.

I stuck my thumb out so much it got cold and sore, and it felt as if it was going to drop off. Just about to give up, I was able to get an old couple to stop. They asked me where I was headed. They were like angels sent from heaven, and who knows . . . ? They took me to their home, fed me a delicious meal, gave me a comfortable bed, and took me back to the highway in the morning. What a blessing!

I have found, however, that trials follow blessings. By next evening, I had progressed to the New Mexico-Texas border and found myself standing out in the blazing sun for hours. Cars sped by, but no one was stopping. As the hours went on, I was getting tired more and more. I left the highway and walked to a couple of stores and houses lining the road. I wearily looked through a telephone directory and called the first church I could find. I asked whoever answered the phone if he could help me with shelter. The man told me that I'd be welcome to sleep on the church floor, but I'd have to walk there–a distance of about five miles. Needless to say, the idea of walking five miles on a strange Texas highway didn't really appeal to me. I thanked him and hung up.

Walking back a few yards, I saw the cafeteria was about to close for the night. Behind the restaurant was a storage shed. There was a whole bunch of stuff in there, and the only thing that looked hopeful and at least halfway restful was a piece of fiberglass. So that was how I spent the night.

I got up early the next day (Surprise, surprise–fiberglass isn't my first mattress choice.) and headed to the highway. A trucker soon stopped and gave me a ride to Phoenix. By this time, I was starving. Without my asking, the trucker shared his sandwiches with me.

I really saw the Lord's hand in this. In my position now as Joy Junction's executive director, I insist that we provide adequate transportation to pick up people. I have also instructed my staff to see that guests who come in late and hungry are fed something, no matter what time of the day or night it is. While I definitely didn't enjoy these experiences, if I hadn't gone through them, I wouldn't have appreciated how tasty a bologna sandwich could be when you haven't eaten for a long time. If that church hadn't offered me shelter five miles away, I wouldn't have understood how distant and hopeless five miles sounds when you're exhausted.

Friends bought a bus ticket for me from Phoenix to Flagstaff. For the next few weeks, I stayed in Cameron, a little village on the Indian reservation about fifty miles north of Flagstaff. I spent a lot of time thinking about Sylvia while I was (I guess) "finding myself." She was back "hanging in there" in Florida, hoping, praying, and believing that things would work out for me somewhere so that I could get a job and send for her and the boys. As if being homeless wasn't enough, she was also pregnant with Jeremiah, our third son.

A few weeks later, on a wing and a prayer–really more of a whim than a prayer, though God honored the whim–I travelled to Santa Fe, New Mexico, the site of the infamous and bloody prison riots. I heard that the penitentiary was hiring prison guards, and the pay was good. I arrived in Santa Fe, also known as the City Different, on a Saturday evening. That night I stayed in a hotel, and the following morning I made my way to Christian Life Fellowship, at that time pastored by someone who not only became my pastor but a close friend as well, Carl Conley.

Another really amazing event was about to happen. Following the service, a church member offered me a place to stay for a week, and then I stayed in the basement of another church member, a local landlord named Rudy Rodriguez. Rudy put me to work painting apartments for him, which as time progressed must have taken a great deal of faith on his part, as I think I put more paint on the floors than I did on the walls of his apartments. Consequently, even long-suffering Rudy decided it would be best if I looked for another job.

A local hotel hired me, and I worked there for a while washing dishes and driving the van. During this time, Rudy and the members of the Santa Fe chapter of Full Gospel Businessmen's Fellowship collected money for me to bring my wife and family out from Florida to Santa Fe. Sylvia was about eight months pregnant with Jeremiah.

Sylvia arrived a few weeks later. New Mexico provided a big climate change and a culture shock after living in Florida. While we were glad to be together and have a roof over our heads and a job, it wasn't easy living on minimum wage. Still, we were luckier than many Americans.

Change

Change was in the air again. My boss came to me one day and said that the owner of the hotel had just paid a visit and had decided to make some staff reductions. I was one of those included in the reduction. Sylvia was less than thrilled when I arrived home and told her that I'd been laid off. It almost looked like a repeat of the Florida situation. No job meant no money, and that meant no place to stay.

However, before the layoff, one of the managers approached me and said he thought it was a blessing for me that I had lost my job. Seeing my look of amazement, the manager explained his comment by saying he felt the Lord was opening the way for me to go into full-time ministry. I wasn't really enthusiastic about this, thinking how easy it was for this man to say when he still had a full-time job to support his family. I had a growing family, including a brand new baby, and no job.

Then I began to think about God's call on my life and wondered if this was the time for me to go into full-time service for the Lord. But with what? Definitely not my good looks. I started thinking about a coffee-house type of ministry where I could preach the gospel. If I was serious, then I'd better start looking for a building. While walking around Albuquerque one day, I ended up in an older section of town, lower Agua Fria. I found a shopping strip comprised of three bright pink buildings. One was a barber's shop; a second was a doctor's office. The store that interested me the most was closed and dark; it had plexiglass windows with holes stuffed full of newspapers to fill the cracks.

I went into the barber shop to see what I could find out. The barber told me that though the empty building was rented, it was only used a couple of days a week. He gave me the man's phone number.

The next week, I went with Carl to meet Toby, who ran some sort of a private club at weekends. Toby agreed to sub-lease to us and, thinking he was being very kind and accommodating, said that if the project didn't work out it was OK. We could stop leasing any time we wanted. While I was appreciative of Toby's helpfulness, there was no question in my mind that it would work.

"His Place" started as a coffeehouse, at first open only for a few hours each evening. I didn't really know at that time what I wanted to do, other than tell people about Jesus. One night I sat in His Place for hours before anyone came by. About nine thirty in the evening a truck stopped by, and I heard some men saying to someone outside, "Here. Go in there. You're wasted. Get some coffee and sober up before you go home to the old lady." For the next couple of hours I had a (drunk) captive audience to tell about Jesus.

I guess the Lord does have a sense of humor. I wanted to tell someone about Jesus, so the Lord honored my request.

I was getting a taste for ministry and began to enjoy it. We had pot luck suppers every Tuesday, and for a while we seemed to become the Christian revival center of Santa Fe. But then the word spread that we were giving away free food. Consequently, the poor, needy, and homeless started coming in. As fast as they started coming around, many Christians started leaving.

As the months sped by, I decided I'd really like to open His Place for an overnight shelter. But there was a problem. With the main tenant occupying the facility for a couple of evenings a week, that just wasn't possible. So I prayed, asked the Lord's help, and for once in my life, left things in the Lord's Hands.

Learning Time

We opened up at night. Back in those days, I was still very naive and thought that if you gave homeless people a place to stay and a meal, then they'd automatically be grateful. It never occurred to me that people wouldn't be thankful for something free, and they might even take advantage of you. But my first phone bill showed that *some* homeless and poor people wouldn't think twice about taking advantage of you. My "crash training course" was in progress.

As the months and years went on, His Place gradually assumed more and more responsibility for taking care of Santa Fe's homeless. The Santa Fe daily newspaper, the *New Mexican*, published a wonderfully descriptive article about the shelter, written by free-lance writer Douglas Conwell.

> The aim of His Place Coffeehouse is more than physical fare. It also includes spiritual fare. The "His" is Jesus, and the message is that "He" can change lives and give hope to the lost and forlorn. Today, the bright pink building on Agua Fria Street is more than a coffeehouse, although that's how it got its start in July 1982. Now its a residential shelter for eight men, with a companion women's residence nearby–one of the few resources of its kind in northern New Mexico.
>
> His Place was the idea of a transplanted Englishman named Jeremy Reynalds, who heard the "call of the Lord" to come to America. Reynalds arrived in Orlando, Florida, in 1978, with $50 in his pocket and a sense of mission in his heart. He worked a number of odd jobs, married, and then moved in with his wife, just cruising about looking for some place to happen.
>
> It happened in Santa Fe, where he was offered a place to live and found employment. It didn't take him long to recognize a "desperate need" for services to the homeless; but he also recognized that as a relative newcomer, there was also a need to establish his own credibility.

Within a short six months, however, Reynalds was serving the ministry of his church, Christian Life Fellowship, through the ministry of the coffeehouse. Reynalds credits the help of several people, including Blackie Gonzales, president of KCHF-TV in Santa Fe, and owner of KDAZ Radio in Albuquerque. Gonzales offered Reynalds half a day's free air time on radio and all the income he could earn from selling advertising spots. Enthusiastic conviction made him a successful salesman. Meanwhile, moral (and later financial) support came from Pastor Carl Conley of Christian Life Fellowship.

First only open for a few hours a day for coffee and doughnuts, His Place remodeled and opened as a shelter for homeless men in November 1983. A similar sized women's residence opened recently. Together, they accept a large number of referrals from police, social services, churches, mental health centers as well as city and state offices. And with at least somewhere for the homeless to go, the possibility of their causing trouble is reduced. As Reynalds said, "Somebody cold and hungry is more likely to steal than somebody well fed."

Not just the homeless come to His Place. There are some area families who are faced with the choice of either eating or paying the rent. They come to His Place so they don't have to make that terrible decision. As Reynalds said, "We help anyone we can in any way we can. We figure if we're going to be in the neighborhood, we'd like to help out."

Being neighborly has been a priority, as some of the nearby residents were not sure about the location of a shelter in their area. Reynalds makes a special effort to communicate and cooperate with these neighbors, and keep the area clean and well organized.

His Place does much more than just feed and house people. Of course imparting the message of Jesus Christ is foremost, and residents are required to attend regular devotional services and other events. But religion is seen in context with a person's life in the community and the feeling of self worth.

Reynalds said that His Place aims to "provide an uplifting atmosphere and to let people know the shelter staff

> loves and cares for them. Our whole aim is to make people responsible. We help them through a transition from feeling broken down, useless and feeling incapable of feeding themselves or working, to being a person who can put a few bucks away and put a downpayment on an apartment.
>
> All residents are expected to find work, but Reynalds tells them, "Hey, I don't expect you to work harder than I do." There's little chance of that–as Reynalds puts in sometimes more than 60 hours a week.
>
> The hundreds who come to the door on Agua Fria have gone through many doors before–doors of divorce, broken homes, alcoholism and drug addiction and aimless wandering from halfway house to rescue mission. Many are in a cycle of poverty, dependent on public assistance that doesn't meet living expenses but is enough money not to give up. Frequently they have been told they are worthless; and most have come to believe it.
>
> The coffeehouse tries to break that cycle with the force of love, but also with rigidly enforced structure. Each person must search daily for employment. "This is not a flop house," Reynalds emphasized. There are plenty of other places for people to flop.
>
> Although the maximum stay is 14 days, Reynalds is flexible. If someone fails to try and improve their situation, they are asked to leave. On the other hand, if a person is making a genuine effort to succeed and just hasn't had any luck finding a place to stay, then he or she is allowed to stay longer.

This article was a great source of encouragement to me, as the author really captured our reasons for being in existence.

His Place provided a training ground for me and cemented God's calling on my life, that of dealing with homeless people. However, in almost four years of running the shelter, I had taken only four days off. In February 1986, my wife Sylvia and I took a couple of days' rest in Phoenix. During that time, I felt God speaking to me about resigning His Place. So I did just that and resigned effective 31 May 1986. Unfortunately, I made a major mistake. I told the Lord that I would do whatever He wanted *except* run a shelter. Never tell the Lord *never*!

The month of May came very quickly. I looked at the possibility of pastoring, but there were no churches available (at least none that wanted me!). My replacement for His Place arrived and expected me to be moving on quickly.

The Almost-homeless Former Shelter Operator

By this time I was really desperate and needed a place for myself, my wife, and family to stay, as our house went with the job. The home-*giver* was about to become home*less*!

I called a long-time friend who lived in Taos (sixty-five miles north of where we were living), and he offered us a place to stay. The experience tested the friendship of both families! After a few weeks, there were still no job offers. I was getting even more worried and depressed. While living in Santa Fe, I had made brief contact with a gentleman who was running a shelter located on Kirtland Air Force Base.

The shelter was called "Reach Out to Jesus Family Chapel" and was part of a now defunct program initiated by the Department of Defense in the days when Casper Weinberger was secretary of the department. The program allowed non-profit corporations the use of vacant military buildings to help the homeless. Don invited me to help him out.

We stayed and helped for a few weeks, but I knew that God had something else in mind. While praying and thinking one morning, I thought of a vacant property in Albuquerque's South Valley. All I knew about the property was that it was large and formerly used by an area alcohol and drug rehabilitation program operated by Christians. The property had been vacant for some months following the demise of the program.

We went down to the property one morning to see what we thought. I was impressed and made contact with the group that owned the property. I told them I wanted to open a shelter for homeless families, and I'd like to use their property. They said they'd get back with me. I left, not really expecting them to take me seriously, but I didn't know that prior to my application, several board members had already been saying among themselves that a homeless shelter would be a good use for this property.

Change Again

During the period between leaving His Place and where I was now, God had been dealing with my heart about the homeless. Both through my wife and through close friends, He had shown me through His Word that He still wanted me to house and feed homeless and hungry people. However much I might run away from or not appreciate that calling, that was what God wanted me to do.

A few weeks later, I received a call from the board telling me that they'd accepted my proposal. I was ecstatic. The terms were reasonable (At least, looking back on it now, they were!): a week's free rent on a trailer for my family and five weeks free rent on a ministry building for the homeless; after that, the rent would be $650 a month. While that wasn't a lot of money, it still seemed like a whole bunch. Anything is a lot when you don't have much. The word poor can be a relative term.

We moved on-site. I was extremely grateful that we all had a home again. The trailer wasn't splendid, but it was home, and we were not required to share it with anyone.

I rapidly became extremely busy. Looking back, I can see God's hand on the shelter right from the beginning. There are several reasons why. First, I had begun the shelter in response to what I believed was God's calling on my life. Secondly, the timing was right. Shortly after I left Reach Out to Jesus Family Chapel, it closed. A small shelter for families run by the Good Shepherd also closed, making Joy Junction the only specifically *family* shelter in the entire Albuquerque area.

Since I started the shelter, my philosophy has been to complement the services of the already existing agencies and never to knowingly compete with them. As such, Joy Junction assists homeless and abused women both with and without children, homeless couples both with and without children, homeless single men who have the custody of their children, and a limited number of homeless men who need a place, for example, to recover after being released from the hospital. We have a number of excellent men's shelters in town. Since I always want to cooperate with them, why should I compete? There are enough poor people around for every agency to have some.

The shelter grew and grew and grew. With this growth, our income also grew. Shelter income climbed from $11,000 the first year to about $45,000 to $62,000 to where, in 1990, the annual income was about $300,000.

The Lord blessed our efforts, and the shelter gained a reputation very quickly. Joy Junction was often featured on the local television newscasts and in local newspaper articles. My skill was definitely in the generation of publicity and attention for the shelter. (Although in times past, I had done everything from keeping the books to teaching many of the regular evening Bible studies.) However, the financial end of the shelter began to get away from both me and those staffers doing the accounting. I knew the shelter was getting in the hole financially, but I didn't know what to do about it. There were bills owing and staff salaries that couldn't be paid, and I saw no way to get out of our financial bind.

Crisis

The pressure seemed to get heavier and heavier. So much so, that I felt I just couldn't take it anymore. I decided the only solution was to go public with the problems the shelter was facing. I announced publicly an ultimatum that if at least $20,000 wasn't raised by the end of the next month, that I would close Joy Junction. This wasn't necessarily the best thing to do. However, at the time, I was absolutely desperate and couldn't see any other way out. Various local television and radio stations publicized the need, and some additional finances started to come in. Maybe things were looking up.

However, I hadn't even seen the beginning of where things were headed. A lot of troubles, trials, and trauma lay just a few weeks ahead of me. *The Albuquerque Journal* called, and it became immediately apparent that this wasn't going to be a light, fluffy report detailing the shelter's need, without any questions asked.

The next week, I spent long hours with a staff reporter from the *Albuquerque Journal.* It was evident from her line of questioning that this was the beginning of a very detailed story. This reporter was going to tell the community *why* the shelter was in its financial bind, and I was going to be held accountable for everything that had happened. You see, this reporter wanted to see a "budget" to see how we had gotten in such a financial bind. Budgets were foreign to me. I had been so busy raising money to pay bills, answering telephones, signing in homeless people, the idea of a budget had never even occurred to me. I had a lot to learn, and since then I've continued to learn a lot.

That's a major reason for this book. You see, I had the best of intentions, and that old expression is true. The road to hell is paved with good intentions. Or more accurately in this case, good intentions just don't cut it when you're dealing with the public's money. You have to know what's expected of you. And at that point, I didn't.

The reporter concluded her first session by asking me if I had copies of the shelter's *990,* an IRS document non-profit organizations are required to submit each year to the Internal Revenue Service. I referred her to the shelter's volunteer bookkeeper, never dreaming what would come out of that simple referral. A few days later, the reporter called me to request a second interview session. The questions went something like this: "Jeremy, can you tell me about the bounced checks and the unpaid payroll taxes for the shelter?"

My heart sank. How did she know? The volunteer accountant had told her. I never told him he shouldn't, and my sending the reporter to see him had made him think that he was to honestly answer any questions that were asked of him.

I decided there was only one thing to do. As she continued to reel though a list of problem areas, my response was something like the following: I looked her right in the eyes and said, "Leah, the public is tired of hearing excuses and seeing the blame put on someone else. As head of Joy Junction, I take the blame. Many of our problems and inefficiencies are due to an excessive work load on my part and an organization that has grown incredibly fast—maybe too fast."

The next few days I was contacted numerous times by the reporter as she added to her story. Needless to say, I was apprehensive, concerned about exactly how the story would be worded. I rushed to get the newspaper each morning, wondering if that morning was going to be the day.

Saturday morning, I ran to get the paper and hastily opened it up. It was worse than I thought. There right at the top of the main section was the worst picture of me I had ever seen and a long article headlined "Joy Junction runs by seat of the pants finances."

After letting the article sink in, I dragged my way to the office. The phone started to ring. Many calls were supportive; some were disgusted and angry, but one call seemed to sum up the thrust of many of them: "You've done too much for too many with too little for too long. It's time we came forward and helped you."

The article showed me many things. People whom I believed were real friends totally ignored me after that. Some people who I never thought cared came forward and offered prayerful and financial support. One of those who stuck with me through everything and encouraged me during one of the worst times in my life was Gino Geraci, at the time associate pastor of Calvary Chapel of Albuquerque, now pastor of Calvary Chapel of South Denver. Carl Conley also made himself available to me immediately as he had been for many years, and agreed to step in for as long as I needed him, and to become board president.

In retrospect, many people told me afterwards that the reason they continued to support the shelter was because I had admitted full responsibility. While some of the things for which I was blamed were not directly attributable to me, in one sense they were because I was leader of the ministry. "The buck stops here."

Months later, when the same reporter from the *Albuquerque Journal* interviewed me again, she also told me the reason she had believed me was that I hadn't attempted to hide anything from her. I had been open in all of my answers to her very probing questions.

At no time was I or any of the members of my staff ever charged with lack of integrity or questionable actions. As I stated in my admission, the main problem was being too busy to oversee everything effectively.

Now the Lord does turn everything to the good if we let Him. The final result of that article was the expansion of our shelter board and the Lord's gift of a business manager, something I had needed for a long time. *The Albuquerque Journal* later put it like this: "Joy Junction has bowed to the inevitable, and put its financial affairs under the watchful eyes of a business manager." In fact, I sometimes joke with my business manager, calling him "the inevitable."

Since that time, as a result of admitting to our mistakes, praying, expanding our board, continuing to use successful marketing techniques, and formulating a budget, the Lord has been very good to the shelter. Our budget has increased to $612,000 yearly, and we retained all of the community's confidence that we might have lost as a result of the negative press and regained the trust of former supporters.

Joy Junction has become a major Christian social force both locally in Albuquerque and statewide throughout the New Mexico area, and we are looking ahead to a bright future. We have recently added fifty-six beds to the shelter–a story that is a miracle in itself.

A Joy Junction Thrift Shoppe has been added and has been a great blessing ever since it opened. We've found that the key to success for a shelter thrift store is to have a good manager. The board's only policy directive was that the store had to pay for itself. We weren't going to subsidize it from the shelter's general fund, one good reason being that we had no money to do so. Now we still give away necessary clothing to residents, but a shelter manager gives the person (or family) a voucher for the items needed. They take the voucher to the store, give it to the store manager, and redeem it for the needed items. In that way, they still keep their dignity, because they're treated like paying customers. Our store is going so well that the shelter is in the process of opening an additional one on the same basis. It has to pay for itself.

If the Lord has given you a burden to care for homeless people, in fact, people of any kind, whether they be alcoholics, drug addicts, unmarried pregnant ladies, or just folks needing a pastor, I pray this book will help you translate your calling into reality, stay on the straight and narrow, and still keep the excitement of your initial calling.

Chapter Two

Stories of Homeless Families

Homeless families are the fastest growing segment of the homeless. Sadly, homeless family shelters are not keeping up with the ever-increasing need for their services.

While there is no typical homeless family because all families are made up of individuals and thus different, during my seven years of running Joy Junction, I've seen a number of characteristics that *are* common to many homeless families. What follows is as much of an accurate picture as I can portray of a typical homeless family. This first portrait of a homeless family is a composite look. That means the Wilson family doesn't exist. I've taken many of the most common features I've found in homeless families and woven them into the Wilsons.

Let's visit the home of the Wilson family: Robert, Cindy, and their three children, Matthew, seven-years-old; Rebecca, five-years-old; and JoAnn, two months old. The Wilsons live in Joplin, Missouri, and have no idea that they'll soon be living in Albuquerque, New Mexico. In fact, if you asked them where, they'd probably answer, "Where in Mexico?"

It had been a worrisome day for Cindy. Only three months before, the plant had cut Robert back to twenty-five hours a week, and there were rumors that he might be laid off, along with one hundred others. Twenty-five-hour paychecks had quickly wreaked havoc with the family budget—so much so that although it was only 11:00 A.M. on this particular day, there had already been three calls from creditors asking when they could expect payment on long-overdue accounts. Cindy began to feel that panicky feeling in her stomach. She had no idea what they were going to do.

The door opened, and footsteps along the hallway interrupted her thoughts.

"Robert! What are you— ?"

"Honey, I've been laid off."

"Oh no, what are we going to do?"

"I'll file for unemployment, and look, I know we'll make it. We've got each other. We've got to."

The next three months flew by. While unemployment was keeping the wolf away from the door, that was all it was doing. There were no frills, just barely enough to pay the rent and the utilities. Robert and Cindy had always paid their bills promptly and had good credit. Now their credit report was shot. The creditors continued to call. The pressures continued to mount. The once free-and-easy relationship between Robert and Cindy became tense and then bitter. Cindy began to blame Robert for the family's financial problems.

One day, Robert was overcome by deep depression. Slumping into his favorite easy chair, he turned on the television. The phone rang, and Cindy answered.

"Robert or Cindy Wilson, please. This is Bill from the NCI Mortgage Company."

"This is Cindy."

"Cindy, we know you're going through a hard time, but we are a bank and not a welfare agency. Unless you can come up with two of your three outstanding mortgage payments, we'll be forced to foreclose in thirty days. I'm sorry."

Cindy hung up the phone in a daze and rushed back into the living room, where Robert was still sprawled before the television. She spewed out a flood of words that she really didn't mean.

"Robert, how can you sit there when we're about to become homeless? If you really loved me and the kids, you'd be out there looking for work. Why haven't you found a job yet . . . ?"

The torrent of words continued. Robert got up slowly, scowled at Cindy, and left the house, slamming the door behind him. Cindy ran to her bedroom, flung herself down on her bed, held the pillow for comfort and wept bitterly. What had she said?

The hours dragged by with no sign of Robert's return. At suppertime, Rebecca innocently said, "Mommy, where's daddy? I heard you yelling at him."

"Sweetheart. . . ." Cindy's emotions began to rise, and she struggled to control herself. "He'll be back soon." With each word, Cindy lost more of her temper, and her voice rose higher and higher. Rebecca burst into tears and was quickly joined by her brother and sister. Cindy ran to her bedroom, grabbing two-month-old JoAnn on the way and left the other two bewildered and scared children in the living room.

At 1:00 A.M. Cindy woke to a crying baby. She comforted JoAnn as best as she could and ran to check on the other children. They were huddled on the couch with tear-stained faces—fast asleep. Cindy gently placed her children in bed and returned to an uneasy sleep. She was awakened two hours later to a sheepish Robert crawling into bed. She reached for him and managed to say between sobs, "Honey, I'm so sorry." They fell asleep in each other's arms, weeping in the midst of a situation over which they had no control.

Robert and Cindy woke early after a nearly sleepless night. They prepared breakfast and sent Matthew to school. Rebecca was still sleeping, and JoAnn was gurgling happily. There was time to talk, drink coffee, and get a head start on the day.

Robert spoke first. "Honey, this just isn't working. I've tried, you know I've tried . . ." He started to weep, and Cindy put her arm around him for comfort.

"We could ask my mom and dad . . ." Cindy said.

"No way!" Robert broke in. "They were always against us getting married anyway, and they'd love for us to break up.

Anyway, they live in public housing and can't have anyone stay with them for more than a few days." Robert suddenly had an idea. "Honey, a few weeks ago when I was out with the guys, we were just shooting the breeze, and they said there's welding work in Albuquerque, New Mexico. We could . . ."

"I'm not going to Mexico," Cindy said.

"No, silly," Robert said. "New Mexico, not Mexico. New Mexico's in the United States, stuck between Arizona and Texas. Let's check into it."

The next few days brought a continued barrage of calls from creditors. Robert and Cindy didn't even bother to answer the phone anymore. What was the point, anyway? There was no money to pay the bills. And then a few days later, they didn't have to think about the telephone anymore. It was turned off.

One evening, a friend of Robert's came to visit. The conversation quickly shifted to money, or the lack of it.

"Rob, I know there's work in Albuquerque. Welders are getting paid seventeen-and-a-half an hour. The housing's cheap, and there's plenty of it. Why don't you guys just pack up and go? What you got to lose?"

A determined look came over Robert's face. "Man, I can't stand this anymore. Cindy, let's do it."

Cindy suddenly recalled something that filled her with more hope than she'd had in the last few months. "Honey, one of the girls I graduated with from high school moved to Albuquerque. I haven't heard from her in years, but she lives somewhere close to downtown there. I know we could stay with her."

Over the next few days, the Wilsons sold most of their belongings, packed the rest in the dilapidated family station wagon (the spare family car, the other one having been repossessed), and set out to Albuquerque. They left Joplin with $350 cash in their pockets.

About an hour after they started, the radiator began to boil. A few miles later, there was a loud pop, and the car sputtered to a noisy halt.

Robert got out of the car and groaned. There were two flat

tires, the radiator was still boiling, and the tailpipe had fallen off. He gave Cindy the bad news.

"I'd better hitch to the nearest gas station," Robert said wearily. "We didn't allow money for car repairs, though."

Five-and-a-half hours and a tow truck later, the Wilsons were on their way again, two hundred and fifty dollars poorer. Robert said glumly, "There's no way we'll make it to Albuquerque on the money we have left. But let's fill up the tank, get as far as we can, stop at the cheapest motel we can find, and think."

By nightfall, they'd covered another two hundred miles, including a brief stop for bologna, mayonnaise, and bread. After checking into a motel, they talked.

Robert said, "Honey, we'll have to stop along the way. I'll work, and we can stay in missions."

"Missions!" Cindy said, half-frightened and half-angry. "No way! We're not staying in any missions."

"Honey, we might have to," said Robert.

The conversation continued on how the family could best make their way to Albuquerque.

The following morning, after more bologna sandwiches, the Wilson family was on the road again, with $32 and a full tank of gas. Nothing was resolved in the motel room discussion, because nothing *could* be resolved. The family expedition lasted three weeks; there were several arguments on the way. Robert and Cindy said many hurtful things to each other in the heat of the moment, and the scars from those hastily spoken words would take many years to heal.

During their trip, minor needs turned into major nightmares. There was no money to buy diapers, and the air conditioning didn't work. Finally, Robert and Cindy saw the signs on the highway they'd been waiting for: "Welcome to Albuquerque." They hugged and wept for joy. At last! Their long ordeal, they believed, was over.

"Let's go to 12th Street, N.W., "Cindy said excitedly, "and we'll find Mary. I know where she lives. Look, I've gotten the last letter she wrote me, back in 1985, and it says the address right here: 1415 12th Street, N.W."

The family made their way to the address with much anticipation, but there was no house or apartment, just a parking lot. After asking around, they found no one who even knew who Mary was. After tears of bitter disappointment, a few inquiries into the Albuquerque job market convinced Robert that there were no welding jobs currently available. The entire family piled their way back into the car and cried. The Wilsons just sat there, too tired and drained to do anything other than cry–and sit.

Seven hours later, a police officer asked them if he could help. Hearing their story, he said, "There's only one shelter that will take you at this time of night and let you all stay together, and that's Joy Junction." An hour later, Robert, Cindy and the children arrived at Joy Junction.

Because of the shelter's structure, Joy Junction is able to help many families like the Wilsons and provide them shelter that keeps their entire family together during such a crisis. However, shelters like Joy Junction are still in the minority. Can you imagine how families like the Wilsons would feel if they had to be split up? What would it do to them?

I hope you're getting an idea by now of how important family shelters are and how we as Christians are biblically obligated to provide more shelters like this one. I reiterate that what you've just read is a composite of a homeless family. While the Wilsons don't actually exist, I drew from characteristics I've noticed about homeless families over the past ten years and put them into one family.

The following are actual case histories. I recently distributed, in a non-random, unscientific manner, a questionnaire to the residents staying at Joy Junction. The questions asked for name (optional), family size, highest educational grade reached or any college training received, home state, what work the respondent has been trained to do, and what work they are currently doing.

I then requested details about how they became homeless, why friends and relatives were unable to help them, how they feel about being homeless, how they ended up in Albuquerque and if they plan to stay, and what they would feel like if their family had to be separated in order to stay in a shelter.

Here are some of their responses. The only thing I have changed is names. No attempt was made to verify any of the following information. It's exactly as we received it.

Jane obtained her GED in prison and has also completed two years trade school. Her home state is New Mexico. Jane is qualified to do commercial driving, computer data entry, and computer analysis, among other skilled jobs. Jane has been doing all sorts of temporary work but mostly cleaning and general unskilled labor.

Here's the story about how she became homeless.

> At a certain point in my life, I had some trouble with the law over worthless checks. It was an election year, so I was convicted quickly and subjected to the full penalty of the law (42 months in New Mexico Corrections Department).
>
> During this period of time, I finished high school and entered college. I had high hopes for reintegration into society. Upon leaving prison, I found it difficult (impossible) to find work because I had to disclose my parole status. I checked out schools and found that I couldn't use any credits from prison as a base to continue my education. I had to begin over again at an accredited school.
>
> I finished my training and also my parole. I was still unable to pass checks by prospective employers because of my conviction. I did menial jobs when I could find them. I was promptly fired in most cases if any hint of my criminal record came to light.
>
> Pretty soon, I couldn't pay rent anymore. I lived in my car till it was vandalized to the extent that it no longer provided shelter.

Jane continued to tell why her relatives were no longer able to help her.

> When a person has been convicted of a crime, by the time they leave the Department of Corrections, they no longer have supportive families and their "friends" are

> often not friends, but often other ex-cons worse off than themselves.

Jane described what she feels like being homeless.

> It feels somewhat humiliating because there are a lot of general misconceptions about homeless people, i.e., that none of them want to work. That they are lazy, and thieves, etc.
>
> There is a stigma attached to the term homeless, and people don't realize that any kind of disaster could render them in the same position regardless of careful planning. It is degrading to make people discover this about you because it alters their opinion (of you) the moment they become aware of the fact.

Many people think that most or all homeless people are transients who aimlessly float across the country. Jane was born in Mountainair, New Mexico. She talked about a common shelter practice–separating families.

> I am currently not living with my husband because he is in the corrections department, but if we were together, we would prefer living in our car to being separated. To me homelessness is a temporal living condition that is hard to overcome because of financial setbacks and job search problems. I would not stay in a women's shelter while my husband was forced to stay in the streets, car, or another shelter. I would stay with him until it is possible to rent for ourselves again, regardless of the circumstances.

Jane had an interesting perspective on the need for more family shelters to be built around the United States.

> I think there should be more shelters built, but I also feel because of the immense concern over homelessness that it is important to make the public, and especially the church congregations, aware that their interaction and help (not financial, necessarily) in counseling, fellowship, and job opportunities is vital to the successful rise of a family from the despair, isolation, hopelessness, and depression of homelessness.

Steve and Maria have one child on the way–Maria is seven

months pregnant. Steve says he has an associates' degree in English, and "my wife has a 6th grade reading level, but supposedly graduated high school." Steve's home state is California, and Maria's is New Mexico. Steve says he is trained in sales, cooking, cashiering, a little computer programming, data processing, and typing. He has been doing a little cooking and cashiering.

In his words, Steve told how he became homeless: "We tried to make it in California, but I was unable to find a job. The money she [Maria] got from welfare for her pregnancy wasn't enough to live on, so we lost our place."

Steve said that while relatives did what they could, it still wasn't enough. "Most of my friends were unable to help because their homes were full or their parents wouldn't allow them to." He painted a graphic picture of the horrors of homelessness. "It's really terrible. I don't know how I'm going to take care of my wife and my soon-to-be-born child. I don't know from one day to the next if we're going to have a place to stay or food to eat. I feel absolutely helpless and worthless because I can't provide for my family."

Steve said if things work out in Albuquerque, "we'll be staying for a while." Asked how he would feel if his family had to be separated to stay in a shelter, Steve responded, "I wouldn't like that at all. My wife has a history of medical problems, and I would be afraid that something would happen. I would sooner sleep on the streets where I could keep an eye on her, than stay in a shelter, separated, where I couldn't."

Steve stressed the importance of more family shelters being built around the United States: "The number of homeless families is growing, but there is nowhere for them to go. In my home town in California, there are no shelters for families, and few for men and women, other than the battered women's shelter."

Every person we asked said they would not stay in a shelter if they had to be separated from their family. Minnesota-born Tracy was no exception. She said it would be too lonely to be separated from her family, and she just wouldn't do it. "I'd sleep when I could, and travel when I had to, but no shelter" (if she had to be separated).

Tracy has had two years of college and is trained in technical-electric assembly. She's currently receiving social security disability and said she became homeless through a drop in her income. Illness caused her to quit working and start receiving social security.

"Through Social Security," Tracy said, "my income dropped to half of what I was bringing in per month. I had to move, to compensate for the lack of money, to an apartment which was a lot smaller and cheaper than what I was living in." Tracy still wasn't making it, so she came to Albuquerque because friends told her there was cheaper housing and an overall lower cost of living than in Minnesota. "So I saved my money and drove here in two days."

"Homelessness is very depressing," Tracy said. "I miss my home and things around me. Just to brush my teeth seems a chore because I have to dig through everything to get my toothbrush. Then if there is room at the sink even to get it done, I get angry very easily over little things, because I can't even have a minute to myself. Everyone needs a little space to call their own."

Tracy said that while she has relatives, they couldn't help her because they're on limited incomes. "They're retired but maintain their homes as they're paid for. They can't afford to have one more person to feed." She said it would be a blessing for everyone if there were more family shelters around the United States.

David and Karen moved from Big Springs, Texas, to Albuquerque, for entirely different reasons–their eldest daughter's health. David is a high-school graduate, but Karen left school in the tenth grade. They have two daughters. David's home state is Texas, and Karen is a native New Mexican. Through his most recent job in construction, David says he's willing to do "anything possible."

There were simple reasons for moving to Albuquerque, David said. "For my daughter's health. We can get more help for her here. She's handicapped with epilepsy, and Texas was overmedicating her." David and Karen said relatives couldn't help them out of their plight, and they don't have any friends in Albuquerque.

Homelessness is depressing, David said. "No privacy, but thankful we have a roof over our heads, meals for my kids, and a place to sleep." Asked if he would separate from his family in order to have a place to stay, David said he wouldn't. "My girls need both of us, and we need them." They agree that there's a need for more family shelters around the country "because there are a lot of families that need the help and shelter."

Sam and Deborah don't have any children, but they both graduated from high school. Sam is a truck driver, and Deborah works in factories and kitchens, but both have been unemployed for the past year. They said they became homeless through divorce.

Sam said that neither friends nor relatives were able to help them because "neither one of us get along with our families very well, and most of our friends couldn't help." The couple said it's hard to be homeless, but there have been some very nice people who have helped them along the way.

Deborah said that Sam's former employment resulted in their coming to Albuquerque. "Sam used to drive a truck through Albuquerque, and he liked the town so we decided to move here. Yes, we are planning to stay." Sam and Deborah said they feel it's important that there be more family shelters built around the United States, as many states don't have shelters where the whole family can stay together.

David and Jean were also residents at Joy Junction. Dennis has a ninth-grade education, and Jean is a high-school graduate. They're from Texas and have no children. Dennis said he's trained to do landscaping, sprinkler-systems repair, construction, paint and body work, and plastering.

Jean recounted how they became homeless: "My husband lost his job at El Paso because the company went out of business. We lost our apartment through lack of money." She said they stayed with friends for a couple of days until they made enough money to buy bus tickets to Albuquerque.

"We got in Tuesday and went to the Rescue Mission, and they told us about Joy Junction. We called, and they came and picked us up. The people here are very nice and also very polite and understanding and caring." Jean explained why they couldn't get any more help than they did from friends. "I didn't want to stay there because they were into drugs." Their family in El Paso couldn't help them because they're already supporting other children.

The couple came to Albuquerque "to stay and get a good job and start a new life here." Jean said, "It's scary and horrible to be homeless because living out in the streets you could . . . trust no one out there. . . . People are getting mugged in front of the El Paso Rescue Mission and the Salvation Army. . . . We are very thankful for Joy Junction having us here."

Jean believes there are more job opportunities in Albuquerque than in El Paso, and the couple plan on staying here. "It will take time, but with God's help we are going to get back on our feet again," they said. She said she believes it's very important that more family shelters be built in the United States to give homeless families with children a safe place to stay.

So are you beginning to get the picture? The vast majority of homeless families aren't "bums." They're people just like you and me who need a break or a second chance. Have you noticed also that most of those who stay at Joy Junction would not stay in a shelter if they had to separate from their loved ones? Now we can say whatever we like about that, but it's a fact.

Have you also noticed that every respondent said there's a need for more family shelters, and they wouldn't stay in a shelter if they had to be separated? There's an untapped mission field out there of homeless, hungry, hurting, and desperate families who are waiting for someone to show them the love of Jesus Christ in a tangible way–so many homeless families, and so few shelters that meet the need.

Obviously, the fact that you're reading this book says you have an interest in and concern for the homeless. Is God continuing to work on your heart even now? As you continue through this book, be very careful. It might result in you making a life-changing career decision.

Chapter Three

The History of Shelters

It's important that you try and get some idea of why shelters exist, what they are, where they come from, and who they serve.

Shelters have been around now for so long that we tend to take them for granted. Many of our neighbors might not like them, but they still accept shelters as a normal part of American life.

In William Seath's book *Unto the Least of These . . .*, in the chapter on the history of rescue missions, it is written that in ancient times, there were groups of people commonly referred to as migrants or vagrants. These individuals were mostly runaway slaves trying to make a new life for themselves in the big cities and stay as far away as possible from their former masters. Rome was a great center of attraction for runaways.

There were also travellers, minstrels, travelling monks–maybe similar to the Methodist circuit riders of the last century–and also those folks who maybe just had the travelling bug, who wandered around the known world. These people earned a precarious living, entertaining or performing some sort of menial tasks along the way. We'd probably call it day labor today. They stopped along the route to work just long enough to get enough money to take them onto the next city.

Thinking about this brings a Bible verse to mind, that the poor we shall have with us always. It's also true that human nature never really changes. During the eleven years I've directed homeless shelters, I've met people who love to hop on freight trains. That's where they get their kicks. And then I've met people who don't want to settle down. They just want to travel from city to city–but they don't care how they get there.

Seath also writes that outside of the Children of Israel, most nations took little or no interest in the poor and unfortunate, accepting their sorrow and misfortune as a way of life. In Jesus' time, even many Jews didn't pay much attention to the poor and needy beggars, as we clearly see in scenes like the pool of Bethseda and the treatment of beggars and lepers who sat at the temple gate. Seath offers the story of Lazarus in Luke 16:20-21 as an example of this: "And there was a beggar called Lazarus, who lay at the gate of a wealthy man. Lazarus was full of sores, and even the crumbs which fell from the rich man's table would have made him happy. Lazarus was so bad off that the dogs came and licked his sores."

Seath continues to note that years later in Europe, many monasteries opened their doors to wanderers such as I've described above. Monasteries gave these individuals food, shelter, and other services–almost like a modern social service agency!

In England, poverty became so great that in the 1600s eighty thousand people were classified as "vagrants." In 1602, King James I issued a proclamation ordering that vagrants be deported from the country. Shortly afterwards, buildings known as workhouses were established to care for the indigent, handicapped, aged, and crippled. According to many reports, conditions in these places were incredibly bad.

The United States' oldest rescue mission was founded by Jerry McAuley in 1872; however, even prior to that, the problem of the homeless was growing rapidly.

Seath says following the Civil War, many men began moving around the country. This has happened in all post-war periods. Men grow restless. After having been uprooted from their homes at a young age, they see new sights, sounds, and places. While they are subject to strict military discipline, they tame the urge to wander. Upon release from the military, however, they feel a great sense of freedom, and remembering all the new experiences they had in the military, they desire to see all of these places on their own. Many times this newfound freedom takes a hold of them and becomes a way of life.

Shortly after 1865, the railroads sensed there would be future growth in the west, and they started expanding the amount of track they had available. This resulted in the railroads needing more temporary laborers, men who were to form the nucleus of the transient seasonal labor movement. As large farms opened, and road construction became a major industry, the need for transient workers increased by a tremendous amount. Adding to the need for these temporary workers was the great increase in the lumber industry and ice harvesting. Transient laborers reached a three-and-a-half million peak in about 1926.

Seath says the majority of these temporary laborers were homeless; that is, they had no permanent residence. Many had limited education, and many came from poor families. As with everything, there were notable exceptions. Among this huge army of people were alcoholics and drunks. All of these individuals were prime candidates for service and ministry by the rescue missions of the day.

In his article "Beyond the Stingy Welfare State" (*Policy Review*, Fall 1990), Marvin Olasky says that poverty fighters one hundred years ago were more compassionate–in the literal sense of "suffering with"–than many of us are now. Olasky adds that these individuals opened their homes to deserted and abandoned women and children. They offered jobs to travelling men who had abandoned hope and most human contact.

Most importantly, Olasky writes, these poverty fighters made moral demands on those whom they helped. They didn't allow those who received their kindness to just eat and run. They saw family, work, freedom, and faith as central to our being, not as life-style options.

How times have changed! Joy Junction and other shelters, both in Albuquerque and nationwide, are criticized many times for having some mandatory church attendance. However, remember that if God has called you to start and run a ministry, that is what it is first–a ministry. While on many occasions Joy Junction is referred to as an "agency" in the sense that we perform social service functions, we are a ministry first and an agency second. Our most fervent desire is to see a hungry "sinner" come in and leave a well-fed "saint."

A major reason for my including this brief overview of the work of rescue in this book is that you need to know the heritage of the work which you are considering. In addition, many Christians today sometimes forget the works and lives of those who have gone before them. That's really a shame, as we have so much that we can learn from them. So remember your history!

Olasky says that the work of compassion about a century ago was carried on in at least as squalid scenes as we can imagine in today's worst barrios. Thousands of orphans roamed the streets, and the infant mortality rates were ten times the present levels. New York Police Commissioner Thomas Byrnes estimated that there were about forty thousand prostitutes working the city of New York in 1890. A survey conducted about the same time found 6,576 New York slum families living in tenement "inside" rooms, that is, rooms that had no windows facing out. All these rooms had airshafts, which many tenants used as garbage dumps.

Yet during this period, Olasky writes, a successful war on poverty was being waged nationwide by many thousands of local charitable agencies and religious groups around the country. These groups were often small and made up of volunteers led by poorly paid professional managers. Much was written by the journalists of the time on how effective these volunteers were. Olasky concludes that the charity workers of a century ago were successful because they were inspired by seven ideas that recent welfare practice has abandoned. They are

- AFFILIATION–emphasizing the restoration of broken ties to family and friends;
- BONDING–forging long-term, one-on-one contact between a volunteer and a needy person;

- CATEGORIZATION—using "work tests" and background checks to distinguish between different types of applicants;
- DISCERNMENT—learning how to say "no" in the short run so as to produce better long-term results;
- EMPLOYMENT—requiring work from every able-bodied applicant;
- FREEDOM—helping the able needy to resist enslavement to the charity of governmental or private masters;
- GOD—emphasizing the spiritual as well as the material.

It's fascinating to me that this apparently very effective way of operating is now almost completely foreign to the way that most social service agencies operate. Olasky writes that during the last century when individuals with real needs applied for material assistance, charity workers began by interviewing applicants and checking backgrounds with the goal of answering one question: "Who is bound to help in this case?"

Case notes from the files of the Associated Charities of Boston read that when an elderly widower applied for help, "the agent's investigation showed that there were relatives upon whom he might have a claim." A niece was unable to contribute, but a brother-in-law who had not seen the old man for twenty-five years promised to send regular financial support. The individual made good on his promise. The brother-in-law's contribution paid the old man's living expenses and reunited him with his late wife's family. The charity caseworker said that if there hadn't been a diligent investigation, all the old man would have received would have been some food. His living situation wouldn't have improved but would have only had a band-aid applied to it.

The last principle of the covenant so vigorously used by last century's charity workers was an emphasis on God, religious faith, and duty. A charity magazine of the time wrote that true philanthropy must take spiritual as well as physical needs into account. The magazine wrote, "Poverty will be dramatically reduced if the victims of appetite and lust and idleness . . . revere the precepts of the Bible and form habits of industry, frugality and self-restraint."

Unwise use of resources is a great problem for homeless people. There is really so much to be learned from looking at how the great "rescuers" of yesteryear used to conduct their business. Some time ago, I looked at a family walking through the door of our facility. This family was loaded down with sodas, chips, goodies, and disposable diapers. Now nothing wrong with that, you might say. I'd agree with you, *if you're not homeless*. But the objective of staying in a homeless shelter is to save as much money as you can, in as short a time as possible, and get back on your feet as soon as you can. That family didn't make it and eventually ended up leaving town. But I can't help wondering, if we had made them more aware of the principles of last century's rescuers, would they have made more of a success of their lives?

Now all of us make choices, and the homeless are no exception. As you're reading through this book, and you're contemplating policies for your shelter, keep the policies of last century's rescuers in mind. But also remember that we are faced with a much more complex world and way of living than they were. For example, so many more homeless families are broken and blended families.

Late nineteenth-century American Christians who read the Bible regularly did not see God as a sugar-daddy who merely felt sorry for people in distress. *They saw God showing compassion while demanding change*, and they attempted to do the same.

St. Vincent de Paul, the Catholic charity, is a name probably familiar to many readers, and in their magazine from about one hundred years ago, they wrote, "The Vincentian must be prepared to discipline, admonish and encourage . . . [Most of the poor] must be disciplined into providence, for they are seldom provident for themselves. To be their true benefactor, the visitor must admonish them to know and appreciate their high destiny."

Groups like the Industrial Christian Alliance reminded the poor that God had made them and had high expectations for them to "restore the fallen and helpless to self-respect and self-support." That's why it's so important for us as Christians to know that we really do have the edge on the world in helping the poor and needy.

While we can attempt to teach the poor and needy the importance of education, the need to be responsible, the necessity to regularly get up for and go to work, what's really going to help is a change of heart. That is, all the help that we can give the poor is secondary to them coming into a relationship with Jesus Christ. They have to learn godly responsibility, and Jesus Christ will give them the reason and the motivation to do so.

As the 1890s progressed, there emerged what is called the social gospel. Leaders of the movement were convinced that real charity must be both universalistic and unconditional. According to Olasky, part of this new thinking was based on a changed view of the nature of God and the nature of man. The older view saw God as both holy and loving; the new view tended to mention love only. This new view saw man as naturally good and productive unless he were put in a competitive environment that, as Olasky put it, "warped finer sensibilities." In this new way of thinking, to put people to a work test (i.e., if a man doesn't want to work, then he shouldn't eat) was cruel because a person who has faced a "crushing load of misfortune" shouldn't be faulted if he doesn't choose to work.

These new thinkers believed that challenging a person wouldn't bring change, but change would only occur when man was placed into a pleasant environment that could bring out his "true, benevolent nature."

It's very important for you to understand these views because proponents of the social gospel tend to criticize evangelical shelter operators. If you intend to require families who stay at your shelter to attend gospel services, then you will definitely face criticism for a variety of reasons, including changes that you are "infringing on their rights."

So you see that it's good that you know the history of charity work, where it came from, how it used to operate, and what caused the change to the current method of operation of many agencies.

There is a balance to both ways of thinking, and Joy Junction has been roundly criticized by advocates of both approaches. Joy Junction is criticized by the social gospel movement for requiring attendance at religious services and for our thinking that man's nature is depraved and sinful. But many of those who support our theological stance fail to understand the dynamics of homelessness when they come down to visit the shelter and observe many of our guests "sitting around." They fail to understand the reality of clinical depression, how it can render someone totally unable to work. They fail to see that homelessness and its associated problems didn't happen overnight and, in all probability, won't be cured overnight.

So what I'm saying is that there's a lot that we can learn from history, but there's a lot that we can learn how not to do from history as well.

Families with children still provide relatively uncharted territory in the rescue movement, so there is no precedent or historical experience to offer help. In every case you'll need to be guided by the Holy Spirit directing you on the individual situation. History can and will give you some good underlying principles and lots of common sense, but always treat every person as an individual. Never do or not do something for a person or a family just because that's the way it's always been done or not done.

The Necessity for Balance

As with most things, most people tend to go to the extremes. I want to hit the balance. So while the rescuers of yesteryear did many things right, I believe there were some things they did that weren't so good, and we can learn from the compassion of the social gospelers without throwing the baby out with the bathwater.

As the progression of the social gospel wore on, many began to argue that only the government could create an economic environment that would save all. What in effect these people did was take away Jesus as Savior and substitute the government.

The belief became popular that really compassionate people

would automatically rally behind the creation of new programs, and some even believed that the governmental construction of housing projects would bring about the new day. Of course, what they forgot was that before any real and lasting improvement can come about, man's heart has to be changed. Give a pig a palace, and he's still a pig, but put a king in a pigsty, and he's still a king. Changing the environment can help in human terms, but it doesn't bring the long-lasting sort of social change for which humanistic advocates have so long argued.

As the momentum of the new programs began to gather steam, people even began to be embarrassed at the evangelical emphasis of the older programs.

The *Encyclopedia of Social Reform* even suggested that evangelical underpinnings to charity work were wrong because university-educated experts now knew that it was "social wrongs" that caused individual problems, and these problems would disappear as soon as the poor were placed in a better material environment.

Those whose motivation for volunteering was to see souls saved as well as hungry bodies fed and clothed, found the new emphasis frustrating and unrewarding and often quit their charity work. Personal involvement was replaced by the efficiency and consequent, necessary non-involvement of social work professionals.

In about 1926 the transient worker's life changed dramatically. Automation had arrived–the introduction of modern machinery. Thousands of jobs were eliminated almost overnight. The introduction of the combine eliminated thousands of farm jobs, and new techniques in road building caused road jobs to follow suit. Mechanical refrigeration almost eliminated the ice harvest, and there was a rapid change in the logging industry. About the only thing left for the temporary worker to do was work laying track, maintaining the railroads, and clearing the railroad tracks in bad weather.

The years 1929 through 1933 brought the Great Depression, creating larger and vastly different problems for the missions. Entire families became homeless. Many of those looking for help were seeking it for the very first time. In addition, many families were unable to support their children, so a vast number of children as young as seven or eight years old left home to look for work on their own.

At about the same time, a new avenue of service arose for the rescue missions because of the migration of many churches from what is now known as the inner city to the suburbs. All these churches were doing was following their congregations out of the city. However, while many churches vacated the streets, there still had to be someone to fill the void, and in many cases, it was the rescue missions that stepped in. In many cases, those who had moved to the suburbs were replaced by the aged, unemployed or unemployable, and minorities.

During the Great Depression, when millions of people were not responsible for their own destiny, and quite naturally jobs were not readily available, it made sense to many to have lots of governmental programs. Olasky contends that continuing some of the New Deal programs during the postwar return to prosperity then set the stage for our modern welfare crisis. In the fifties, he adds, many poor families remained intact, and (very importantly) most people saw benefits not as rights but as backups for use only during dire emergencies. What Olasky calls the "entitlement revolution" of the sixties he says has not helped the poor. Olasky sums up the overall change in shelters as he sees it between the 1890s and the 1990s.

> To see firsthand, what homeless individuals could receive and were expected to do, I recently spent a couple of days dressed as a homeless person in Washington D.C. I was given or offered lots of material at shelters and agencies, both government-supported and private—lots of food, lots of medicine and lots of clothes (even a bathing suit so I could use a free swimming pool). *But not once was I asked to do anything–not even to carry away my tray after a meal.* (Emphasis mine)

Olasky says that an able-to-work homeless person in 1890 would have been asked to take some responsibility for his own life and to help others as well, by chopping wood or cleaning trash. Then, Olasky says, he would have had to make contact with other people, whether relatives or former colleagues. But today none of that happens, and he is free to be a "naked nomad," going from meal to meal. When anyone suggests that responsibility might help this person, they're told very emphatically that they are infringing upon his rights.

Again, balance is the key word. You must realize that when some people come off the streets to stay at your shelter, they are mentally and psychologically unable to work. They are almost shell-shocked; call it PTSS—post-traumatic street syndrome. Before they can do anything, they need to mentally and emotionally heal. Now, there will come a time, and it could range from a few minutes to a few weeks, when they'll need to work. It might be around the shelter, perhaps as part of a therapy to get them back on their feet again. Your job is to treat every person as an individual and be sensitive to the leading of the Holy Spirit as to how He wants you to minister to them. Learn from yesterday, but don't be bound by yesterday. "Eat the cherry, but throw out the pits."

Chapter Four

Starting Out

So you really want to start a shelter or get involved in the people-helping business? Whether you want to start a homeless shelter, a Christian school, an alcohol and drug rehabilitation program, or a crisis pregnancy center, there are some very similar principles.

One thing required for any ministry is the minister's "call of God." The call of God is more important than it sounds because that "call" is what will keep you going through the hard times.

God speaks to His people in various ways. To some He speaks through pastors, ministers, and priests, to some through circumstances, and to others He might highlight some particular aspect of His Word. When I resigned my first shelter in Santa Fe in 1986, I made the mistake of "telling God" that I would do anything He wanted me to do except run a shelter. I figured I had paid my dues running the shelter in Santa Fe for four years, and now it was time to do something else. I not only told the Lord how unwilling I was to start another shelter, I told Him I wasn't willing to start another ministry–period.

Some of my reasoning behind my fervent determination not to start another ministry was that many times the hours worked parallel the opening of a new business. Outrageous working hours are exchanged for small and often late paychecks.

For your ministry to go anywhere, you have to sell yourself to the community and the local pastors. Your (potential) donors have to believe in you before they'll believe in what you're representing. Before you groan and say that shelter-ministry or people-ministry in general isn't for you, try and understand where pastors are coming from. Ministers (and people in general) receive so much mail asking for money that it would be impossible for their church to respond to every solicitation they receive. It might be said that the strongest survive.

These were just some of the thoughts going through my mind as I kept myself busy telling God what I wouldn't do. Meanwhile, God's plans were not my plans, and His thoughts were not my thoughts. They were much better and infinitely higher. God had eased me into my calling in Santa Fe, but if I'd been smart, I'd have realized that He orchestrated so many special events in my life to give me empathy for the homeless, that He wasn't going to let me out of the calling that easily.

So if you're worried about the step you're considering taking, that's good. Use the questions in your mind as an excuse to pray more, both individually and with those to whom you look for spiritual counsel. If you decide at this point not to go ahead, it's OK. It doesn't mean you're less spiritual than anyone else. It rather means that God has something else in mind for your life. On the other hand, make sure that you're obeying God and not giving into fear. Don't try and wiggle your way out of God's calling on your life like I tried to do.

During my last few months in Santa Fe, I applied as a pastor to a few churches. During the "trial sermon," I told them what I thought the prerequisites for a good church were. A recurring theme in my messages was always ministering to the poor and needy. (I wonder why!) It wasn't intentional. The subject just kept coming up. Evidently what came through in my messages to my potential congregations was that I was more interested in the poor and needy than I was in the spiritual needs of their church members.

Needless to say, I was not offered any churches. So I came to the end of my time in Santa Fe and had no job offers. In desperation, I applied to a foreign missions agency for a job and was accepted. That could have been cause for rejoicing, except that to take the position would have required relocating to Denver, and the job was a "faith position." In other words, I had to raise my own salary. I attempted to raise some money, but nothing happened. It seemed to be all me doing it, with no help from above. I felt like I was fighting my own battles. Life was getting very discouraging.

That's what happens when you fight God's will and you're not willing to listen to the still, small voice of His Holy Spirit. God sometimes ends up having to hit you over the head with a spiritual two-by-four. On the other hand, don't run into ministry because you think it's sort of romantic or cool. Running a shelter and ministering God's love is some of the hardest work that you'll ever do in your life. And no one thanks you except God.

It's very hard to describe God's calling because it is such an intangible and personal experience. In many cases the calling of God almost defies written description, but I'm going to try by relating some more of my own experiences, which will hopefully help you as we go through this adventure together.

While my family was staying in Taos, on several occasions we visited good friends of ours who formerly pastored a little church in Questa, a little village community about twenty-five miles north of Taos. While visiting these friends, we also had several occasions to go to the mountains to pray.

Talk about God orchestrating things. My friend's name was Frank Tercero; he was at that time a pastor in the Assemblies of God. Little did I know that four years later I would meet Frank at a mutual friend's home in Santa Fe, and Frank would be looking for a job. The Lord used Frank to bail both me and the shelter out of a mess when we had received the unfavorable publicity in June 1990.

During those prayer times, the Lord brought Scriptures to my mind again that my wife Sylvia felt the Lord had given her concerning our future life and direction. Frank also had words of encouragement and direction. Those words confirmed what I was already feeling but had been unwilling to face up to. God wouldn't let me out of my calling.

It's very rare for God to use other people to speak to you about a situation or a calling or a change in calling that He hasn't been speaking to you about already.

There have been situations when people have "received" and acted on directions to quit a job, sell everything, and move to a far corner of the earth, e.g., Alaska. God hasn't been speaking to them directly, and neither has He nor they been preparing their hearts. They listened to erroneous advice from others that masqueraded as a "word from God." I urge you to be very careful about that.

The Scriptures that the Lord used that fateful year included verses from Isaiah 41,

> The poor and needy search for water, but there are none; their tongues are parched with thirst. But I the Lord will answer them; I, the God of Israel, will not forsake them. I will make rivers flow on barren heights, and springs within the valleys. I will turn the desert into pools of water, and the parched ground into springs.

While the Lord was able to speak gently to Sylvia and others that serving the hungry and homeless was still where He wanted me to be, it really took something more drastic on my part. He had to continue to engineer the circumstances and take every other opportunity away from me before I would finally give in and say, "Yes, Lord. I'll do what You want." The Lord will do whatever it takes to get your attention to listen and obey His calling. He'll woo you and be very gentle initially. But if you're quite determined that you're not going to obey Him, then you give Him the freedom to resort to other measures.

The calling that God has on your life will also be confirmed by others in your fellowship or church body. In all probability, if God has been dealing with you about starting a shelter or entering some form of people ministry, it will be an extension of a call already upon your life.

What I mean by that is while the spiritual calling of God is sort of intangible, it will in most cases coincide with tangible physical circumstances and actions.

Hopefully, in most cases even before reading this book, you'll have had some concern for the poor, needy, and dysfunctional whom you see around you. Perhaps you've been encouraging your pastor and your church to do more for the hungry and homeless in your community. Perhaps you've been taking homeless families into your home who call the church asking for help. Maybe you've been taking food and blankets for the homeless downtown. Or perhaps you've had a real concern for all the alcoholics you see wandering around town. Or maybe there's no Christian school in your community.

A real calling from God will transform your life. It'll allow you to keep your mental, emotional, and spiritual sanity when it looks like everything is going to come crashing down around you. A calling from God won't make you arrogant; it will give you peace.

Don't forget something that many Christians both forget and ignore. If you know that God has called you to do a job, while it's up to you to do everything you can to ensure success, ultimately the final responsibility for the operation lies in God's hands. Another reason why the calling is so significant is that where God leads, He feeds, and where God guides, He provides. Remember that during this whole process, while you're trying to find, define, enhance, and refine your calling, *keep praying*. God knows and isn't necessarily impressed with the enormity of the need. God is impressed with your obedience (or otherwise) to the area of need which He tells you to meet.

Getting Your Wife on Your Side

If you're married, tell your wife. I couldn't be any more serious when I tell you that ministry of most kinds–especially the kind when you go out and start it yourself–will probably demand a dramatic change in your schedule and quite possibly your paycheck. Spousal support is very important since ministry will change your whole family life. (It's like having a new baby in the house!) Is your spouse willing to put up with the excessive hours you'll initially be gone from home, quite possibly for some years into the future? Be realistic about this, not hopelessly overoptimistic. Spousal support is also an indication of the will of God.

Will your wife have to obtain outside employment for a while (if she hasn't already) to make even basic ends meet? Is your family, not only willing, but able to reduce its standard of living? If you're heavily in debt, this might be the time to stop right now and, rather than attempting to start a shelter, look for one already in existence and offer your prayerful and financial support. Of course, you should start reducing your debt load as well. (Smart Christians do this regardless of the call on their lives.)

If your wife isn't initially thrilled when you first share what you feel God has been speaking to you, don't give up, or write your wife off as being unspiritual. Don't make any rash moves at all, but keep praying. After all, if the burden you have, say, for the homeless comes from the Lord, and He managed to get through to you, He can also get through to your wife to turn her heart in favor of the project. Remember, it's the Lord's responsibility to turn your burden into reality.

Telling Your Pastor

Make an appointment to see your pastor. Tell him honestly and as simply and clearly as you can how you feel that God's been speaking to you. Ask your pastor to tell you truthfully what he thinks. Be willing to listen to what your pastor says. He sees things about you and your family, both strengths and weaknesses, that you might not see.

If you don't have the sort of relationship with your pastor that allows for a counselling session like this, then find someone you can trust who knows you and is willing to tell you both your strong and weak points. Ask them all to pray for you. Among other things, you'll need prayer for wisdom, guidance, and God's favor.

Start to meet regularly with your pastor and/or those whom you have praying for you. While there is a chance that God could deal with you in a manner similar to me (where you have no job, but God still has to force your hand to get you to do what He wants), it's more likely that you'll be leaving a job where you've been relatively well-established and might be earning a reasonable income. You'll need all the prayer power you can muster.

If you're thinking about leaving a good job, there are some people who'll think you're crazy. Are you? Maybe. Could it all go wrong? Possibly. If after receiving all the right signals you still don't go ahead, you'll probably never be totally happy and fulfilled again. There will always be a nagging doubt at the back of your mind about what your life might have been had you launched out in faith and obeyed God.

Also tied in with the will of God is the community need for the ministry you feel God has called you to. Consider employing an informal community survey. For example, if you feel God has called you to start a Christian school and there's already one in the area, please make sure that you visit with the school already in existence. Don't be a maverick, doing whatever you think. The best way to spread fear and rumor is to operate in secret and isolation.

Communicating (Oh, It's Important!)

You should make appointments to meet with the directors of already established agencies and ministries in your city and let them know what you believe God is telling you to do. Make it clear to these individuals that you're not planning to compete with them (That would be foolish anyway.); you are rather intending to complement their already existing and excellent service.

Allow me a word of caution. Sometimes Christians are very free in their use of "evangelical jargon." And when we talk in evangelicese, no one else knows what we're talking about. If you're at the zoning office for an official appointment, don't talk spiritual lingo. Be polite, official, courteous, to the point, and leave.

It really is very important that already existing agencies hear about your plans from you and not from someone else. There's a tremendous fear of the unknown among human beings, and you'd be surprised at what the image of your proposed homeless family shelter could quickly become once it has travelled through half-a-dozen people. Before you know it, someone will be claiming that you intend to be the only shelter in town and close down everyone else. (Or you might be accused of planning to begin a cult!) Gossip is not based on common sense.

Reassure any fearful agency heads because, unfortunately even in the people-helping business, there's sometimes some territorialism. As you speak to other agencies, use a soft approach. Tell them that you're concerned about the lack of family shelter, Christian schools, alcoholic rehab, etc., available in your city and ask them how they would feel about an additional agency in the city targeting the specific need which interests you. Hopefully, such a meeting will turn out to be a very positive experience, allaying any fears that you're a maverick trying to sneak in the back door trying to do something behind their backs. It could also serve as a good reference point for leads to attain an adequate property for your proposed shelter, school, church, and so on.

Property and Zoning

Finding adequate property that is correctly zoned could well turn out to be one of your most difficult tasks. There's a really good chance for discouragement to set in during this process, which is another reason why it's so important to have a call of God you can stand on. With a genuine call of God, discouragement can turn into an opportunity for God to prove His greatness and power to you.

Joy Junction has been exceptionally fortunate in property zoning issues. The property the shelter occupies is a seventy-two-acre farm in Albuquerque's south valley that was formerly used as a Christian alcohol and drug rehabilitation center. I didn't realize when I began looking into this property how God had been going before us preparing the way. It was about a year after the shelter opened when I found old press clippings from DARE (the name of the center that occupied the property before Joy Junction came into existence). One story stuck in my mind, reading something like this: "Angry Residents Protest Influx of Drug Addicts Into the South Valley."

The property's former zoning status was *A-1*, an agricultural zoning. Despite the protests of the concerned residents, the then-county commission decided to grant a special use permit (*S-U*) for the life of the property. The *S-U* reads that permissible activities on the property are educational, rehabilitational, and religious. We have been thus blessed with a zoning classification that many mission directors only dream about.

Neighbors

During the years that Joy Junction has been in operation, we have only had occasional neighbor problems. I guess our neighbors are more willing to have homeless families in their neighborhood than they were to have recovering drug addicts. Now if you're sheltering, say, homeless families as opposed to homeless men, you'll have the sympathy factor on your side. Homeless families–in particular, homeless children–tend to generate a lot more sympathy than homeless men. Use this factor to your advantage.

However, when there has been a (potential) problem with our neighbors, I've taken care of the situation quickly. I've also assured our neighbors that we're as interested in their welfare and safe and enjoyable standard of living as we are in that of the homeless.

Some time back, I also invited our neighborhood association to meet on site. I felt it would help allay any fears that they might have about the shelter. The fear of the unknown is one of the best causes of gossip, so I thought that if I invited them on site and they could actually see the homeless, then they would realize that the homeless are normal people just like you and me.

As you look for property, pray and look, look and pray. Ask your church to help in the search, go to those who are praying for you, and consider joining one or maybe two civic support groups like the Kiwanis or the Civitans. These groups are always looking for both worthy projects and good speakers.

Don't expect your search for suitable property to necessarily resemble mine. God works in an infinite variety of ways.

You see, my experience in finding property in Santa Fe was very different to my Albuquerque experience. In Santa Fe I quite literally had to tour the city on foot (I had no car.) to find a suitable property. We also experienced frequent complaints from neighbors who didn't appreciate having a homeless shelter as a neighbor.

For Joy Junction, I thought about the old DARE property, did a quick tour of the facility, put a proposal in to the landlords, and awaited their response. A few weeks later, a favorable answer came, and we moved on site. If you don't find a building at first, don't give up. If this is God's project, He has to provide the means for you to accomplish it.

Financial Support (for You)

While looking for a building, you also need to be considering support, both to finance the ministry and to provide for yourself and your family. Please don't ruin your family in your desire to help the homeless. Countless divorces are caused by fighting and squabbling over money. You need money to survive, and it's not unspiritual to admit it.

If you're planning to get into caring for homeless families, please do it responsibly. Don't blame God for crazy ideas. I get embarrassed to be a Christian sometimes when I hear some of the crazy things for which God is blamed. When I started Joy Junction, I had no reserves of money, but I did have part-time employment working for a local Christian television station as a master-control operator. That put bread on the table and covered some basic needs.

The Bible says that if you don't take care of the needs of your family, or make no effort to do so, then you're worse than an unbeliever. Don't do something flaky like quitting your job and having no tangible means of support to fall back on. That approach is stupid and just brings reproach on the Kingdom of God. It might be an excellent idea even now to analyze your income and expenditures, look for every way possible to cut back, and then save the difference.

A few weeks ago, I was reading a story about a company that just expanded to the Albuquerque area. This is their fourth or fifth store, and their volume of business is now so big they were able to obtain outside financing to start up in Albuquerque. But it wasn't always like that. When the chain originally started, the couple who started the company pushed the limits on their credit cards and self-financed their dream. They invested their own personal resources to turn their dream into reality, as well as putting in many long hours. While not necessarily advising that you play the risky game of pushing the limits on your credit cards, I think you see the analogy. What the world is willing to do for business you must be willing to do at least as much, and hopefully more, for the Kingdom of God. Here's another way.

Find a wonderful loving pastor who has a heart for seeing people responsibly move into ministry. When I started His Place in Santa Fe, I was a newcomer to the community with no credibility. Pastor Carl Conley told me that as I contacted churches, people, and organizations in my attempt to solicit support, I could use both his name and the church name to gain credibility. His kindness was really an instant trust builder.

If someone in the community is kind enough to do that for you, please don't let them down. Make sure you honor any promises you make to anyone.

How Do You Ask for Money Nicely?

Be prepared to write letters to people asking them for money. If you can write an acceptable letter, you'll be way ahead of many agency heads who have to hire outside consultants at high prices to perform that service. If you've never written such a letter, it may be a good time to get your feet wet by signing up for a writing course at your local community college or university. I was loaned the money way back in 1986 for our first mailing. I wrote about three hundred letters and received one response of $300, enabling me to pay back our postage loan and write an additional letter, generating some more funds.

I also stayed on the phone a lot, calling everyone I could

think of and telling them that there's a new shelter in town. "So please give us a call if we could help out." As word of our existence spread, people began referring needy clients to us. I also received a few invitations to speak, which generated a little more income.

Let me remind you again. Be prepared to work long hours with little expectation of reward. Keep your personal expenditures down to a minimum.

Ask your pastor for permission to share with your own church. Maybe your pastor will give you the opportunity to briefly share your dream with the congregation for a few minutes one morning. The church might even end up taking an offering for your proposed work and send you out with their blessing.

How Much to Pay for Your Ministry Building

You start looking and finally find a building that appears as if it might work. You call the zoning inspector, who tells you that this just happens to be one of the few buildings located in an area of the city that would permit a homeless shelter, an alcoholic rehab, or maybe a homeless meal site. You're in luck. (If you're looking for a building for a church, you shouldn't be having all of these problems, so I won't be offended if you skip the rest of this chapter and go onto the next one!)

You make an appointment to go see the landlords; be entirely honest with them. If they don't mind the idea of their building being used for a homeless shelter, then it's time to talk money. Work out a rental or lease agreement that you can afford. Just as credit cards eventually have to be paid for, so lease and rental agreements also have a day of reckoning. If you can't afford the price of a building, don't rent it. Please don't "faith it", i.e., take on the responsibility for a building that you have no hope of affording and one where you will end up being consistently late paying the landlords. All that does is reflect badly on you and the body of Christ in general.

So now you have your building. I can't emphasize strongly enough that you must be prepared to do everything it takes for as long as it takes to ensure the success of your shelter or chosen ministry. While you as a Christian have God's blessing if you're operating in His will, there are still no shortcuts to success. God's will plus God's blessing plus hard work equals success. Leave out the hard work, and the success just won't be there.

As we prepare to wrap up this chapter, I'm assuming that you've been communicating in some way with those already in some sort of people ministry. As you get together with these folks, bring up the idea gently and courteously, in a non-threatening manner, about the ministry you feel God has laid on your heart. Communication is the name of the game.

Be prepared to start off small. Many people want to start off big and grow even bigger, but God's way is for you to start off small and to see what you do with what He gives you. As God sees you faithful in little, He'll reward you with more.

There is definitely no magic formula for launching out in ministry. The advice I'd give you for supporting yourself in the initial stages would be very different from person to person, depending on your family size and whether you already have some other means of outside support. There are some things you can do, and those are what I've tried to lay out in this chapter–necessary regardless of your personal situation.

In summary, remember that starting and successfully maintaining a people-oriented ministry is very similar to starting a successful small business. It is time-consuming and emotionally draining. Count on doing everything yourself until the income increases to where you can hire staff. Ministering can be very rewarding, but it's definitely not glamorous. Your only reason for wanting to be in "full-time" ministry should be to obey God's call on your life and to share the love of Jesus Christ with hurting people. If you're thinking about ministry for any other reason, you're probably considering the wrong profession.

Chapter Five

—*———

Nuts and Bolts of Ministry

I'm going to use a shelter as our example of people-helping ministry in this chapter. If you're considering another type of agency, just substitute yours when I mention the shelter.

You believe that God is calling you to be a part of seeing the need for another shelter in your city met. What do you do? I've already hinted at, and I'm sure you've heard all the usual stories about people going off the deep end, quitting their job, and plunging their family into financial disaster.

Don't do that–please! Talk to your wife first; if your spouse isn't in agreement with what you feel God is saying to you, then maybe you shouldn't do it. You definitely don't need to take care of the homeless if it's going to cause a divorce in your own family. After you've talked and prayed things over with your spouse, assuming that you're in agreement, the next person to see is your pastor.

Share with him what you feel God is saying to you and your wife. Hopefully, he will also bear witness to the work that you feel God may be calling you to. If your pastor is in one accord with your "dream," consider asking him if he would call a church meeting of anyone who might be interested in a shelter for homeless families. Such a meeting might go something like this (adaptable to the way meetings are conducted at your particular church).

You call the meeting to order and share informally what

you believe God has laid on your heart. Share your heart, the dream that you have to help provide some physical and spiritual help for hurting, hungry, and homeless women, children, and families.

Remind those present at the meeting of the scriptural obligation that Christians have to take care of the poor and needy. *Then* ask them if they think the time is right and whether you are the person to help alleviate some of the suffering in your town. Ask them to pray about any possible involvement and then call another meeting. At that next meeting, it's time to ask for some level of commitment.

For those who attend and appear both committed and interested, consider scheduling some luncheon meetings over the following few weeks. You may want to ask individuals who appear to be sympathetic to your vision, as well as those with whom you think you can work, to be on your board.

A Board

Board? I can almost hear you saying, "I wanted to minister and help homeless people, not get involved with corporations and boards." Yes, *board*! If you're going to run a successful agency and have the public involved financially, then you must establish a non-profit corporation. You're also going to need tax-deductible status. That means people who give to your organization can deduct the gift from their income taxes.

A non-profit corporation needs a board of directors, and before qualifying or even applying for tax exemption, the IRS demands that you be a state-approved, non-profit corporation with a board of directors. So how do you choose a board? Very carefully and very prayerfully! In fact, if you rush into choosing board members or choose them for the wrong reasons, the situation could turn out to be a personal disaster for you. You could end up being fired by the ministry which you helped start and poured your life into. (Naturally, make sure you also don't end up doing something for which you deserve to get fired!)

Don't be like the founders and directors of some non-profits who gather a group of men around them who served as nothing more than "yes-men." The director or CEO of the organization is never challenged and has complete liberty to do whatever he wants. He just receives a "rubber stamp" of approval on all of his decisions.

That is a definite problem because all of us are fallible. It can be a very constructive process to have individuals around us who will challenge us creatively on some of our choices and decisions. A well-thought out and well-planned decision can only be strengthened by carefully thinking through all the ramifications of that choice.

So surround yourself with a group of caring people who love you and care for you and the ministry, but who will also not hesitate to tell you if they see you acting in an inappropriate manner. As we'll get to later, this means that successful board members must be able to separate their unsubstantiated opinions or biases from situations and circumstances that are definitely wrong and inappropriate. A board must have the faith, trust, and confidence in your management of all the everyday goings-on of the ministry. Even if board members do know of a better way of doing things, if it's a situation that's involved with everyday management, the board must be willing to stay out of things. You do not have the license to be stubborn, proud, and unteachable!

So be very careful about your board members. Especially as you expand and grow more successful, there will be lots more people wanting to get involved. Unfortunately, some of them may think they can do the job better than you can. Even if that's true, it's not the point. If you started the shelter, you're the one, for whatever reason, whom God decided to entrust with the ministry. However, don't abuse the trust that God placed in you!

If I haven't made you panic yet, let me explain a little more about non-profit corporations.

Non-Profits

There are a variety of non-profit corporations, but basically they all exist for the benefit of others. For example, there are non-profits that are geared toward the education of children. There are also those that are established to oversee the rehabilitation and care of developmentally disabled adults. Even some hospitals function as non-profit corporations.

But to become a non-profit agency recognized by your state, you have to have articles of incorporation and bylaws. The articles of incorporation are basically a statement you make to the state as to what you plan to do. They proclaim your "reason for being" and detail how you plan to carry out what you have told the state you plan to do. They are a written outworking of your internal organizational plans.

For example, bylaws give details of how to consistently resolve disputes in your ministry. That means you have an established policy for dealing with disputes. You just don't deal arbitrarily with people depending on the time of day or the month of the year. You deal with everyone the same.

To be granted tax-exempt status by the Internal Revenue Service, you must be a church or a state-recognized, non-profit corporation organized and operated exclusively for religious or charitable purposes. If you're not willing to apply for this status, you're really beginning to skate on the thin, razor-sharp ice of the tax code, which might well break and damage you beyond repair as you sink. Yes, you open yourself to possible inspection of your organization's books by the IRS as a non-profit, but you're also making a public statement that you're willing to abide by the IRS regulations (which you need to even if you don't want to!). Most corporations or corporate foundations to whom you might turn looking for a substantial gift also demand that you be recognized as a 501(c)(3) by the Internal Revenue Service.

Being a recognized non-profit organization—also known as a 501(c)(3)—assures your donors that they may deduct their gifts to your organization from their income taxes without fear of penalty.

Here are some specific details from *Christian Ministries and the Law* by H. Wayne House (Baker Book House, 1992).

> The non-profit corporation is by definition a creature of the statutory law of the state in which the corporation is formed, and includes any corporation whereby

no member, officer or director receives a profit. Most states model their non-profit corporation statutes after the Model Nonprofit Corporation Act, a nationally recognized statutory scheme developed by legal scholars and practitioners, whereby non-profit organizations of many kinds–religious, charitable, scientific, etc. may become legally recognized and defined entities under the laws of the state of incorporation.

The first step to be taken by an organization is to incorporate under this act. This usually consists of preparing articles of incorporation and filing them with the secretary of state, along with a filing fee. If the articles meet all the requirements, the secretary of state keeps one copy on file and then sends back to the incorporators a file-stamped copy of the articles, along with a certificate of incorporation, which confirms the existence of the corporation in the state of incorporation.

Before sending the articles to the secretary of state, however, it is wise to check with the secretary's office to see if the proposed name of the corporation is available. If the desired name is already in use, another will have to be selected . . .

The act has certain significant requirements for the articles of incorporation. Most significantly, they must include the name of the corporation, the period of duration, the address of the office of the corporation, the name and address of a registered agent for the corporation in the state, the names and addresses of the original board of directors and incorporators, as well as the purposes of the corporation. In addition, the articles must be signed and notarized by the incorporator(s).

There may be other reasons for including certain types of additional information in the articles of incorporation. For example, if the organization is going to pursue federal tax exempt status the articles should include language indicating that upon dissolution of the corporation all of the assets will continue to be used for charitable purposes. Individual states may have similar requirements for obtaining state tax exempt status.

After the incorporation process is completed, the next step is to prepare and adopt bylaws. Many churches use the term constitution and bylaws interchangeably. The bylaws essentially comprise the governing rules of the corporation and should cover several basic areas.

"At a minimum, bylaws should cover the following: selection of members; time and place of annual business meetings; calling of special business meetings; notice for annual and special meetings; quorums; voting rights; selection, tenure and removal of officers and directors; filling of vacancies; responsibilities of directors and officers; method of amending bylaws; and purchase and conveyance of property [Richard R. Hammer, *Church and the Law*, Gospel Publishing House, 1983]."

After the incorporation process is complete and the bylaws have been adopted, the corporation then may commence its activities as a newly formed corporation. The non-profit corporation, once it is formed, however, continues to be subject to the statutory framework that was the instrument of its inception. The Model Nonprofit Corporation Act governs many aspects of the corporation. One ongoing requirement is that the corporation file an annual report with the secretary of state, along with a small fee. The report includes completing a form provided by the secretary, and generally reaffirms much of the information contained in the original articles. Any significant change of purpose, for example, would be indicated on the annual report, as would a change in the registered agent, etc. Failure to file the annual report and pay the fee may, in some states, result in an involuntary dissolution of the corporation. Although reinstatement is usually possible after involuntary dissolution, the directors and officers of the corporation should be diligent in following this and all other requirements of the nonprofit corporation act of their state, and seek legal counsel if necessary.

In summary, the nonprofit corporation is the common form of legal entity for religious organizations, including churches, in the United States today.

Once the state in which you live has approved your articles

of incorporation and bylaws, you are now able to apply for tax exemption from the Internal Revenue Service.

Seeking Tax Exemption from the IRS

So what are the requirements to gain you this privilege? Now before we go any further, it is important for you to remember that what I am giving you is only an overview of how to achieve tax-exempt status from the IRS. I am not attempting to provide you with step by step instructions. Having said that, let's proceed.

Your organization must be a corporation operated and organized exclusively for religious, charitable, or educational purposes. The IRS further says that the net earnings of the corporation can't benefit any shareholder or individual. That doesn't mean you can't get paid for working for your organization, only that the agency you've helped create is now becoming publicly accountable, and the ministry coffers aren't your private "piggy bank." Your organization can't endorse politicians running for office, even if they're totally sold on your cause. Now the IRS isn't saying you can't say *anything* about legislation. The wording they use is that a "substantial" part of your organization's activities can't be directed toward influencing legislation. What's substantial? That's where the confusion and controversy arises. If you have to speak out on legislative issues, be very careful and confine your activities toward educating your audience or donor constituency. Present both sides of the issue and let your audience make up its mind.

As someone in the "people-helping" business, you definitely qualify for the intent aspect of the 501(c)(3) tax exemption. I suggest you check with someone knowledgeable every step of the way to make sure you're headed in the right direction. You could also call any of the IRS's toll-free numbers to obtain the IRS Form 1023, Application for Recognition of Tax Exemption.

Now a little bit more on your salary situation. The IRS says your organization can pay you and your staff a salary as long as it's "reasonable." Now what's reasonable? (The IRS seems to enjoy vague wording like "reasonable" and "sufficient," doesn't it?) Reasonable to you and the IRS might not necessarily be the same thing. Let me try and explain. If your organization is grossing an annual income of, say, $250,000 and your personal salary is set at $225,000, I'd say there's a strong possibility that the IRS is going to define that as "unreasonable" should it be brought to their attention. If your organization has gross receipts of say $5 million dollars, and your salary is set at $225,000 then the IRS might well determine that as being perfectly reasonable.

You might be asking why the IRS has to have a stake in your salary. Here's the answer. When you receive the advantages of tax exemption, not paying taxes on the monies coming into your organization, and are also granted the ability to issue tax deductible receipts for your donors, it's a tremendous privilege. If you want the advantages of tax exemption, you also have to be willing to play by the rules and go along with what you might consider disadvantages.

Whatever you do, play by the rules, whether it's receiving a reasonable salary or staying out of or taking a low key stand on political issues that you might be very interested in. Don't play "hero" and risk losing your tax exemption. To the IRS, ignorance is absolutely no excuse at all for violating the law, and the IRS usually wins. They have a whole lot more money and resources to fight a dispute than you do. Be watchful, prudent, and cautious.

I hope I haven't bored you with all this information. I feel very strongly that you should be fully educated about as many of the ramifications as possible that are involved with the outworking of your vision. One of the reasons for the writing of this book is to make sure your God-given vision, not only comes to fruition, but stays afloat. Many well-intentioned people start ministries, but as good as the cause may be they run aground in the first year or so. I want yours to be successful.

Now once you've sent the application forms and all the appropriate paperwork and filing fee to the IRS, pray and leave it in the Lord's hands. During this time, your ministry can be in operation. You just don't have official tax-exempt status yet. Don't call the IRS to ask them what they're doing if you haven't heard within a few weeks. I'd give them at least several months before you make any phone calls.

The day comes, after patient waiting, when that all important "OK" from the IRS finally comes through. You're now a 501(c)(3) tax-exempt organization. Congratulations! But don't wallow in self back-slapping for too long! While tax exemption is necessary and you have done everything legally that you should have done, as I've tried to make clear in this chapter, you're now obliged to conform to all the rules that are imposed upon a non-profit corporation. There are lots of things that you must do and lots of things that you can't do.

More Nuts and Bolts Stuff

Payroll Taxes. Yes, I'm sure it wasn't the first thing on your mind when you entered "ministry." But if you have employees, you need to pay them, and you'll be responsible for payroll taxes (those deductions you've seen on your paycheck for years, before *you* became the employer, remember?).

Depending on the number of employees that your organization has, payroll tax money can quickly accumulate into a pretty sizable amount. Every time you issue a payroll, make sure you set aside the right amount of money to deposit to the IRS account at your bank. It might not seem a lot at first, but if left unpaid it quickly mounts up. *Please, please, please* don't borrow from this money if you run into a cash flow problem.

I know how tight money can be for non-profits, especially during the summer slump months, for example. *But it's not your money.* It is employee money that you need to deposit into their account with the Internal Revenue Service. The IRS is never happy when you either don't pay or you're late in paying your taxes. They take an especially dim view if you rifle the payroll tax deposits. The way not to do that is never to issue a payroll without the accompanying deposit to the IRS.

Not playing by the IRS rules is just not worth it because it's not your money. If the IRS gets wind of questionable handling of payroll tax deposits, they'll be right down on top of you. If the situation escalates, you could ultimately have your organizational bank accounts levied (that means the IRS could go to the shelter bank accounts and order your bank to give them all the money that they say you owe them).

In addition, if your shelter owns land and buildings, the IRS could put a lien on them. Worst case scenario, they could also come down and seize shelter vehicles, furniture, and more to be sold to pay your debts to the IRS. The IRS could also come against the personal assets of your board and financial manager. The resulting publicity would probably close you down, as you'd generate an immediate crisis of confidence among your donors.

If I haven't scared you so far, I do hope that I've managed to let you know what a serious matter it is to be a steward of public funds. Now I know you might not be taking any federal, state, county, or city funds but in the sense I mean, you're still a guardian of public funds because you're being entrusted with donations by a concerned public to do a certain job. That's a privilege and a responsibility. You have thus (albeit unknowingly and maybe even unwillingly) become a public figure. You are open to much more scrutiny than someone who is working, say, in a factory. You are also an ambassador of the Body of Christ, and whatever you do reflects either positively or negatively on the Church. Please don't become a reproach to the Body of Christ. It has suffered enough scandal in recent years.

Probably the most important advice I can leave with you in this chapter is this: Don't go "cheap" on your Articles of Incorporation and Bylaws. I know attorneys are expensive, but if you have to hire one to write all the necessary documents and get them done in both a professional manner and the way you want, then hire one. A few more dollars spent now could save you a lot more dollars and a whole lot of personal grief later.

Do the payroll taxes and all the deductions correctly. If you can't afford or don't yet have the need for a full-time business manager, then think about having the payroll done by contracting with outside professionals. You'll be glad you did. There are multitudinous regulations (and they're increasing every year) that relate to payroll, employer responsibilities, and so on. It takes time to keep up with the changes in employer responsibilities. If you've only skimmed through this chapter, please go back and read it carefully. It is *very* important!

I've merely scratched the surface here and have only managed to deal with generalities. For specific advice on your situation, you need to contact the IRS or a tax attorney. If you see a problem beginning to emerge, deal with it professionally and quickly. Don't wait until you have a full-scale PR disaster. Damage control is easier before than after.

Chapter Six

Zoning

Zoning! The very word strikes fear into the hearts nationwide of shelter directors, drug rehabilitation program operators, Christian schools, and even pastors. Let me tell you my experience.

Joy Junction's main neighbor is the city of Albuquerque sewer plant. Some time ago, while on the phone to that facility's director, we both agreed that while the two of us perform vital services, no one wants us in their backyards. Most people are agreed on the need for shelters, but it seems that many people's attitudes are, "Well, let the other side of town take care of it!"

I was at a city council meeting one day when they were dealing with a mission's attempt to expand its facilities. Neighbors were upset and petitioned the council to deny the mission's expansion request. They said that their area of town was overloaded with services for the homeless, and that additional space for the homeless would result in more homeless people being drawn to the downtown area.

The mission's contention was that rather than drawing more people to the downtown area, that additional space would just enable them to more effectively service the existing homeless population. However, the mission's request was denied.

Lesley Casias of *The Albuquerque Tribune* wrote the following:

> The executive director of the Albuquerque Rescue Mis-

> sion says he is disappointed by the City Council's refusal to approve the shelter's plan to expand, but he has not given up.
>
> "There are no dead ends with God," Mark Fairchild said Tuesday in response to Monday night's 7-1 decision that supported neighborhood protest to the expansion.
>
> The mission, 509 Second St. S.W. in the Barelas neighborhood, had requested an expansion that would increase the number of beds from 32 to 62.
>
> Currently, the mission's 32 beds are completely filled all year. The mission also often shelters between 15 and 30 people in sleeping bags on its dining room floor.
>
> Neighbors feared the shelter's expansion would decrease their property values and threaten their personal safety.
>
> Fairchild said in the five years he has worked at the mission, there has not been a complaint logged by neighbors about the shelter's users.
>
> But Councilor Steve Gallegos, who voted against the expansion, said since his nine years as a representative for the area he has received many complaints about public drunkenness, drug abuse and indecent exposure.
>
> The Tribune added that Gallegos said the complaints weren't about all the homeless people, just a small percentage who ruin things for everyone.
>
> "It's usually the small percent that ruins it for everyone," Gallegos said. (The Albuquerque Tribune, 1992. Used by permission.)

Reason doesn't usually dominate discussions on the homeless, and it's hard to strike a balance. Yes, there needs to be more shelter for men in Albuquerque, but the residents in this neighborhood felt they had almost single-handedly born the brunt of the city's homeless for too long.

As much as the Albuquerque Rescue Mission tried to calmly, rationally, and in a Christlike manner explain that additional assistance for the homeless wouldn't hurt the neighborhood, but rather help, it was all to no avail. At that point, should you find yourself in this same position, as a Christian, you have literally done everything you can. What's left is to realize that success or failure ultimately comes from the hand of God. If He wants a mission or an expansion, He'll have to engineer circumstances to achieve it.

At the recent discussions and deliberations on the rescue mission, there was as much discussion on the overcrowded homeless shelter situation downtown as there was on the presence of another building adding to the homeless. The folks in this particular downtown neighborhood felt "dumped on" by what they saw as an uncaring city that is unsympathetic to their problems.

So where do you go from there? As I mention in another chapter, Joy Junction has been exceptionally blessed by legally correct zoning. The shelter is zoned *A-1*, which is an agricultural zoning, with a special use permit, for the life of the property. The special use designation is for educational, rehabilitation, and religious uses for the life of the property. We couldn't ask for better zoning. But zoning like that didn't come easily. The alcohol and drug ministry that used this property before us had to fight and pray for that zoning exemption way back in the early seventies.

Joy Junction has benefited and is continuing to benefit from someone else's fight to secure this zoning. So how do you find property that is correctly zoned or has the chance of becoming so? You *pray* and *look* diligently.

When I was in Santa Fe, the situation wasn't quite so favorable. We occupied a storefront building in a residential area. The shelter was primarily for single men, who on many occasions weren't quite as well behaved as they should have been.

I made a special effort to understand the concerns of neighbors who had been in the area for many years and who saw a homeless shelter as something to be feared. My philosophy then was the same as it is now: That we are not in an area to minister to the homeless and cause our neighbors to fear, hate, and dread us. Rather we are there to be a blessing to everyone. Look at it this way. If we take care of the homeless and win them to Christ, but we make the lives of our neighbors miserable, what have we gained?

Everyone who has anything to do with shelters must have the willingness and the ability to sympathize with neighbors' fears and concerns. That does not mean letting the neighbors automatically ride roughshod over you, giving in to their every demand. It means being sympathetic and making every possible effort to be a caring, concerned, and responsible neighbor. It also means you remember the neighbors were there before you.

However, to act responsibly doesn't mean all your problems will go away and that your neighbors will think your idea for a shelter is the best thing they have ever heard. They still might not like you. It is your responsibility to make sure that every conceivable avenue where the devil could gain a foothold into God's work has been taken care of. The ultimate responsibility for the success or failure of the project lies in God's hands, but you must help make the success of God's work easier. Don't let an attitude problem give God more work to do.

What I am saying is: Don't have an attitude that says, "This is God's work. I'm going to do what I'm going to do, and the rest of you, in fact anyone who gets in my way, can just go fly a kite." If you have that attitude, it'll probably be you who ends up flying the kite!

If you do have a neighbor problem, and all your efforts still seem to fail, don't get a nasty attitude and give up. Remember who the Lord of the work is. His methods are not ours. Discussing problem situations agreeably over a cup of coffee tends to solve a lot more problems than adopting an ugly attitude and threatening to go to the press because you're doing "God's work." You're neither above the law nor people's feelings.

If the neighborhood, city zoning boards, the board of appeals, etc., see that you want to work with them and be reasonable, it will make a big difference. You still may not get exactly what you want, but at the very least you might end up with some sort of compromise. Should a decision go against you, never, never make ugly comments about any city official to reporters. If you do, it will be a decision that you'll live to regret, quite possibly for weeks, months, and years to come. If you have to say anything derogatory about any city, county, or state official, tell it to the Lord and let Him take care of it. The Lord keeps secrets well. Reporters don't. They're not supposed to.

Sometimes you come to a place where there is absolutely nothing you can do except pray, and while that may seem like a bad place to be in, it's really not. Take the example of the Albuquerque Rescue Mission. I was at the meeting when councilmen denied permission to expand to the mission. The mission director tried his best to make the appropriate arguments in favor of expansion.

It was a fruitless cause. The mission told the councilmen that while they were seeking formal permission to expand from thirty-two beds to ninety-four, the increase wasn't like it really sounded. On many occasions, the mission sleeps about thirty people on the floor in sleeping bags just to keep them out of the cold.

The neighbors complained that additional mission space would bring more homeless people to an area already troubled and overburdened with social services—the downtown area. A number of community members testified that they already had enough problems with homeless people urinating in public, hassling patrons, panhandling, and so on.

The mission's contention was that an expanded facility would not add to the problem, but that it would rather help ease the present problem. One argument ran something like this:

"There is a problem with people urinating around your facility, right?"

"Yes, and a bigger shelter would just make it worse!"

"Why? Had you thought that if these individuals had adequate bathrooms to take care of their personal needs, that they might not urinate close to your business?"

A reasonable argument, right? But not enough to convince some people who had made up their minds that adequate shelter for the homeless would automatically bring more homeless people to the area.

So in a situation like that, all you can do is exactly what was done by the director of the rescue mission. You thank God for the outcome, whatever it is, and trust that there are indeed no dead ends with God.

When you run up against what appears to be a dead end in the search for a building, you keep praying, and you keep on looking. If God is in the project, He'll work something out, and if He isn't, you don't need to be involved with it anyway. Sooner or later, and in God's time, the right facility will be available to meet your needs.

There are no magic answers to finding a building that's right for what you need. The only advice I have for you that will stand good in every situation is pray and look, and look and pray.

I reiterate: Never burn your bridges behind you. Aside from the fact that it's not a Christian thing to do, you never know in the months and years ahead when you'll have to work with the same people you've just offended publicly.

What After the Building?

So let's move on a little and assume that after months of prayer and searching that you've found a building. It doesn't look like you're going to have any (or at least too many) problems with the neighbors, so it's time to start cleaning.

At least initially, don't be disappointed if everyone doesn't think your vision/burden is the neatest thing to arrive since sliced bread. People (yes, even Christians) prefer to board a moving ship. If I sound like I'm being cynical here, I don't mean to be, just brutally honest. People will desert you if you're going down, and they might not support you until you become a winner. It's just a human characteristic–that's the way many people are.

Back to clean-up. You find a building, and the location and the zoning appear to be good. You're excited. (I know you are, because I've been where you are now.)

However, there's a major problem. The building is trashed.

At its best it might be described as a "handyman special" or "a facility with great potential." At its worst, well . . .

It doesn't worry you because you can see it with the eye of faith. You see the children running around a freshly painted nursery. You can see families staying safely together with a roof over their head, warm food in their tummies. You can visualize the counselor's office where, with the help of the Lord, broken families are being put back together again. You take your best friend in (or even your wife), and, for some strange reason, they look at you like you're crazy. Their only response is "Huh?" That's to be expected–at least to some extent.

Don't get mad with them. God gave you the vision. How does that all relate to clean up? You might end up doing the initial cleanup by yourself.

Maybe even as you're reading this, you're thinking: *Me* do all the cleanup by myself? *Yeah, you*! If I could clean up the buildings out here before Joy Junction opened, and I'm the most impractical person you could ever hope to set eyes on, then there's hope for you. However, if you can in a friendly manner corral any family members, friends from church, etc., into helping you clean up or renovate, all the better.

The other thing you might hear is: "Oh, I'm glad that this building looks like it's going to be OK, but had you thought of all the expense involved? Where's all the money going to come from?" And it's at this point that you have to be really careful. While you don't necessarily have to listen to the "Doubting Thomases," you do need to somehow temper faith with a healthy blend of practicality.

Faith and Reality

What I mean to say is don't listen to those who say that you'll never accomplish your vision. Still, don't run after that vision without using common sense.

Avoid running up huge bills you don't have any chance of paying. Remember that it's of no benefit to take care of the homeless at expense to local merchants who are trying very hard to make an honest living. The idea of your plan is not to force local merchants into homelessness because the local homeless shelter is not paying its bills.

The next piece of advice I shouldn't have to say, but I will anyway. *Don't write any "faith checks."* There has been a practice in some Christian circles of writing hot checks (faith checks) and then "trusting the Lord" to bring in the money to allow the check to clear. Trust the Lord for the money to go in the bank account prior to writing the check! One of the worst testimonies is for a Christian ministry to write checks that bounce. You'll get a reputation very quickly in the community that you don't want!

Be a person of your word and pay bills on time. If you run in to some kind of emergency (a real one, not a manufactured one!), and it looks like you'll be late paying for something, let the creditor know. Don't hide from them, and don't say the check's in the mail, unless it is.

If building cleanup and renovation was all you had to do, then your life might not be so complicated. However, remember that building cleanup is only one of a myriad of tasks with which you'll be faced.

You also have to keep an eye on fund-raising and, right in the middle of building cleanup, be aware that you might have to dash off to speak to a group about the pressing financial need you face if your vision is ever to become a reality. You see why I emphasize the importance of being sure that God has called you to this task? There are so many hassles along the way that it's essential to know that you're in God's will.

Being Christlike to Regulatory Agencies

You must keep a good attitude when dealing with the various city and county departments that regulate your shelter. Yes, even if you decide not to accept a dime of government money, you will still be regulated by various local government departments. Before you go any further, you need to reconcile yourself to getting along with these individuals who work for the local government agencies. The way I look at it, these folks have their job to do, and I have mine to do as well. Both of our jobs will be so much easier if we can get along. Most of these agencies will work with you if you act in a polite and respectful manner and show that you're willing to fulfill the requirements that the law enforces them to impose on you.

An example comes from my own experience early last year. I returned from lunch, and my secretary smiled and said, "Guess who called?"

"No telling," I answered, thinking that maybe I really didn't want to know.

"The fire department," she said. My secretary and the majority of the shelter staff were surprised about the call, but they shouldn't have been. Just the previous Thursday and Friday, I had instructed all the staff to do fire checks.

"Why?" they had asked.

"I don't know," I said. "I just have the feeling that something is going to happen, and we need to make especially sure that everything is OK."

I returned the fire inspector's call, and he said he had received a complaint about the shelter and would be down shortly. For emotional support and backup, I also called our board president, who came down to wait for the inspector's visit.

As soon as the inspector arrived, we made it clear real quick to the inspector that we were going to cooperate with all of his recommendations.

"Inspector," I said, "we've always cooperated with you. We always will." We didn't claim any special church or religious privileges; we were just very polite and respectful.

The inspector made it clear that he was willing to work with us as long as we were willing to conform to the fire code and obey his instructions in the appropriate amount of time.

The visit ended up costing us about $25,000. Even if you think what the county fire or health inspector is telling you is absolute nonsense, you are legally bound to obey their codes. And in the end, your facility will be considerably safer and above reproach. Now we could have pitched fits, created all sorts of ugly scenes, and everyone's life would have been miserable. What would have been the point? We didn't and continue to have a very good relationship with the county fire department.

Just because we are a Christian ministry, we are *not* above the law.

I think about how the visit could have been at a less opportune time. The inspector paid his visit in January–just after the Christmas and Thanksgiving seasons, when many people make substantial gifts to shelters–so we had money in the bank. Now granted, it was earmarked for savings to help us get through the lean summer slump, but at least it was there.

So be nice, and be cooperative with the fire department. The same rule applies to your dealings with the health department. Be cooperative. Please, please, *please* don't try to claim any special privileges because you're "doing God's work." You still need to be safe, and the health department is not there to tyrannize your life. They inspect kitchens to make sure operations are safe, sanitary, and hygienic.

These guidelines apply for dealing with every government agency, and they should govern your interactions with everyone.

Being Christlike to Everyone

Dr. James Dobson, Christian psychologist and head of Focus on the Family, frequently encourages his listeners to call legislators on matters relating to family values. I think it's terrible that Dr. Dobson has to remind Christians to be courteous and respectful when they call. We should not have to be reminded of those basic rules of civility that are valid for those who are not even Christians. Courtesy never hurt anyone, and it pays tremendous dividends.

So how are you feeling after this chapter? Discouraged? I hope not. I've tried to remind you about the tremendous privilege to serve God in a full-time capacity, but also to dispel some of the romantic notions that people sometimes get about "serving the Lord full-time." It's the hardest work out there but definitely the most rewarding.

Go forward in faith and obey God!

Chapter Seven

Almost Opening Time

So you're almost ready to open? Now that you're beginning to realize everything that's involved in opening and running a ministry, are you still excited?

The root meaning of the word *minister* means "to serve." It's *servanthood.* It's long, hard hours, and, in many cases, the only one who will appreciate all that hard work, is the Lord *Himself.* Can you see how important it is to have a calling from God?

The following sections mostly apply to the difficulties experienced by para-church ministries, so if God has called you into the pastorate, your situation is somewhat different. You're looking (hopefully) at more of a guaranteed income source because, as a pastor, you'll have the benefit of having tithers (people who give 10 percent or more) to the church. In many cases, that makes budgetary and financial planning a little bit easier. Non-profit operations have to rely entirely on the offerings.

Money–You Can't Leave Home Without It

It's time to look at money. Yes, I know God supplies. I'd be the first to tell you that, but there's also nothing wrong with building and using an effective mailing list. It is not any more wrong to use mailing lists than it is wrong to use money to pay for goods and services that you need. What is wrong is the *love* of money and the *abuse* of mailing lists.

While there's always the possibility that God could supernaturally rain money down on you from heaven, in all likelihood He isn't going to. You—yes, you—are going to have to raise it. Perhaps you're thinking, "But I can't do that." Then you might be in the wrong business. If you can't raise money, then find a good second-in-command who can. But as a founder or potential founder of a para-church ministry, you're probably going to have to spend a lot more time on the money-raising trail than you might at first realize.

Mailing for Money

Back in 1986, I would take every opportunity to speak to any civic group, church, and so on, that would allow me the opportunity to speak. That was a good way to start getting names and addresses of people who were interested in donating to the shelter. Today, whenever anyone brings a donation of food, furniture, clothing, or absolutely anything to the shelter, we give them a receipt with duplicates for copies for both the donor's records and yours. Add that person's name to your mailing list.

After you've been running a shelter for a while, you'll discover that people love to give clothing to shelters. You'll probably be given so much clothing that you'll become sick very quickly of even thinking about it. But before you start turning away clothing, and possibly offending some of your donors, think about this:

You're in a financial bind. It's been a terrible week for donations, and the payroll, which at this time might include only your name (Ha, you're thinking, what payroll!), is a couple of weeks late.

You've been praying, "Lord, please send some money in. Lord, please send some money in . . ." Money is the only thing that's on your mind. You're still trying to believe God, but you're working long hours, not seeing your wife and kids as much as you should. Not only is there no money for extras, there's no money for essentials either. On top of that, you've heard a few kind-hearted Christian friends muttering that if you had *real* faith, you wouldn't be going through your current financial crisis.

Your wife has been real good about it. While she hasn't nagged and grumbled, that's made you feel worse because you're feeling guilty about not providing for your family.

The telephone rings. You answer, just hoping and believing that this could be the phone call. But instead of it being a donor asking if they can bring you a large donation (Well, a donation of any size would be nice.), it's a call from a donor saying that she has a three-quarter-ton pickup full of clothing. Will you be there this morning to receive it?

What do you do? A short-sighted mission director, and that's liable to be one that won't last very long either, will ungraciously turn the clothing down. And do you know what? Turn that donation of unwanted clothing down, and if that person ever comes into some money, you won't see it either.

I took a long way around to say this. I know that your storage room filled to the ceiling within two weeks of your opening your shelter doors and allowing the first homeless family to sleep there. I know that the last thing you want now in the middle of hard financial times is to be charming, sweet, and gracious and to smile pretty to a donor who wants a tax receipt for some clothes, which in all probability she should take to the dump. But you can't afford to wallow long in such musings. You can't afford to be ugly to people.

So you need to grin and bear it. Cheerfully unload all those clothes and make sure you get that lady's name and address before she leaves. Before you write the next letter asking for contributions of money for the shelter make sure she's on the mailing list.

I cannot emphasize strongly enough, use every available opportunity to get names and addresses. Yes, you're a faith ministry, and yes, you're going to believe God for all of your needs. But many faith ministries live or die by their mailing list, and God never said He would not use mailing lists as one of the tools by which He would supply our needs.

Remember, you're not hearing pie-in-the-sky theory from someone who doesn't know what he's talking about. You're learning the nuts and bolts reality of what it'll take to get a ministry on its feet, stay on its feet, and be a good reflection of the name of Jesus Christ in your community.

Let's recap on the ways to start and build a mailing list. Before you take any names, you have to sell yourself and what you stand for (your principles, you as a person) before you can sell what you're doing.

Take every opportunity to speak anywhere you can and get the names of everyone in your audience for your mailing list. When people ask you what you need, don't be afraid to tell them that you're looking for places to share your message.

An additional tip: Both when you speak and when you write, share the needs of your clients–not the needs of the agency. No one wants to hear about the needs of the agency. Maybe they should want to hear about the needs of the agency because if the agency goes under, then your clients needs are going to be unmet. But they don't make that connection, so take it from me: they will more likely respond to the needs of the clients.

On the PR Trail

Carry a notebook with you and get a supply of cheap business cards. Organize some special events that cost you nothing or next to nothing. Let me tell you what we did recently.

The shelter was given over three thousand ears of corn. While thinking about what to do with them, I had a brainstorm. It was getting close to Labor Day, and while our shelter had never done anything special on Labor Day before, there wasn't any reason why we shouldn't start. So we organized a corn-eating contest. We opened the contest to the general public as well as the shelter guests. Some local churches got involved, and a local Christian radio station and a Christian television station provided free advertising for the event.

As an incentive for people to come, I called a local hotel chain and asked them if they would like to provide us with a free room and a free breakfast in exchange for being mentioned on all the advertising connected with the event. I also called Pepsi and asked for free sodas in exchange for free advertising. I faxed press releases to all the local media, which really paid off. Three of the four local television stations sent coverage, and we were featured briefly on the evening newscast. One of the local newspapers ran a small piece in their briefs column, and a local secular news station called me for an interview.

The event was a great success. Some people from whom we hadn't heard for a long time brought donations to the shelter. (Yes, we took down their names.) We were also the only shelter in town doing any special event on Labor Day. The television crews told me that they're always looking for stuff to cover on Monday, especially a holiday Monday.

Seize every opportunity to get your message out to the public. That's the only way that you'll add to your mailing list.

Thanks to the dubious activity of some televangelists and their hard-pitch, "personalized send me all you can and God will bless you" mailing lists, mailing has gotten a bad rap in some circles. However, if you make up your mind in advance that you're going to stick to a high moral standard, mailing is a valid and legitimate tool to help you take care of the people whom God has entrusted to your ministry.

For many years, while we had a mailing list, I didn't fully realize the importance of mailing. I just figured that God was going to supply, which He did. It was just very important that I realized that there were certain things that I could do which would make God's job a little easier.

Mailing and Marketing "Stuff"

There's a balance to be struck in mailing. First, before you can mail, you have to have people to mail to—that's why I've spent all this time talking about ways to gain names for your mailing list.

So the time has come. You've been gathering some names, and you now have to write a letter. You've called some marketing companies. They asked you the size of your mailing list, and when you told them five hundred, seven hundred fifty, or maybe even fifteen hundred, they just laughed at you. Even after they laughed at you, you pressed them a little bit on prices (You told them how great your project was.), and when they told you the price for their services, you nearly fell off your chair. Yes, marketing companies are expensive.

So you're back to your own resources. You're staring at a blank computer screen, and you still have no idea what to say. Did you honestly expect that it would be like this when you started a shelter? (Or a drug and alcohol rehab, or a Christian school?) Yes, you have a wonderful idea, and you're doing God's work, but it needs to be worked and administered just like a business.

Don't skimp on your appeal letters. Make them look professional. Professionalism will pay back dividends many times greater than the amount of money and energy expended on doing so. You don't have to produce full-color, glossy appeal letters. If you attempt to do that, you'll be accused of wasting your donor's money. But if you produce something that looks sloppy, of poor print quality, and you don't follow any of the rules that are used in marketing and fund-raising, expect failure. Your (potential) donors won't want to support something that looks like it's going under. Balance is the key word.

Telling Your Guests' Stories to Your Donors

Take a questionnaire similar to the ones that I used and hand it out to guests staying at your shelter. As you've no doubt found out by now, all of them are very different individuals with very different stories.

Tell your guests what you want the information for and obtain a signed release. Tell them that you'll be happy to change their names to protect their privacy. If you do that when you write the letter, be sure to tell your donors that everything is exactly as you were told, with the exception of the individual's name, which was changed for confidentiality.

Once you have the raw information, you have to put it in a form that your donors want to read. You have to grab someone's attention and make them want to go on reading. You also have to show how your shelter played a big part in seeing that person's needs met. You also have to show them that while it's the shelter that gets all the attention, you couldn't do it without your donor's help.

People give for a variety of reasons. They give out of a feeling of guilt. They give out of what they believe is a response to a command from God to take care of the needy. There are also those who give out of genuine concern for the needy, hungry, hurting, and underprivileged. But one thing that all donors have in common is they want to feel that their gift (of whatever size) counts. They want to feel that they are playing a part in seeing needs met.

Always remember, they are. As good as you might be, you would not have the ability to carry on any sort of work for the poor, needy, homeless, and oppressed without your donors' generosity. Your donors are your lifeblood.

You're still staring at the blank computer screen. You even feel bad about asking for money. I used to, and I made a vow to the Lord back in 1982 that I would never ask for my own needs, but I would ask for the needs of the ministry. Somehow you have to write a two-page letter (or thereabouts) that's going to leap over your reservations, make sense, and touch people's hearts.

Some Fundamentals of Writing Donor Appeals

From the information that you gathered from your guests at your agency, take the most startling statement. It may be something like, "I had no where to stay. I couldn't stay with my relatives, parents, or friends. There was absolutely nowhere for me to go. Then I found_______________ (the name of your agency). They took me in; they gave me a safe place to stay. The people at _______________ are really neat people."

Use that as your opening one or two paragraphs and then place in the following paragraph something like, "While it's true that our agency helped so and so get back on their feet again, we just couldn't have done it without *your* gift. *You* made the difference."

Hopefully letter writing is a skill that you'll grow into. Even if you're not the best in the world, it's still probably going to be something that you'll have to do for a while. Just remember that whatever you do, be scrupulously honest. Relate the story; tell the need; state clearly what your agency is doing to help meet the need; and then ask for money to help meet the need. Don't make any "faith promises" in the letter, such as, "If you give to this ministry, God will bless you, heal you, and your gift will be returned to you a hundred times." And don't be discouraged if you feel you're a dismal failure and you can't do this. I've been doing this for many years now, and I still have a long way to go.

You also need to get a bulk mailing permit as soon as you possibly can. There are various types of bulk mail permits, but the cheapest is for a 501(c)(3) non-profit organization. As of the time of writing, the first-class mail rate was twenty-nine cents. The cost for mailing a single piece of bulk rate mail in your town runs less than eight-and-a-half cents, so you can see the savings. I've discovered that the delivery time for bulk rate is good. Most of the in-town bulk rate letters that I mail out get to their destination the next day.

Personalized letters aren't bad, i.e. those that read, "Dear Jeremy." However, you're probably going to need some basic computer programming instruction if you want to do that. Otherwise, you're going to be back into the game of finding a marketing company that you can afford.

If you're fortunate enough to be able to use personalized letters, stay away from "direct messages from God." I've had letters from evangelists where they claim God told them to write to me. I'm told that their justification is that I'm on their mailing list. God told them to write to their mailing list, therefore God told them to write to me. I believe that tactics like that are dubious at best, grossly deceptive, immoral, dishonest, and evil at worst.

This chapter is not an invitation to neglect prayer. But please don't skip over this chapter and "very spiritually" think that you're going to pray all your resources in. Do everything that you can to ensure the success of your ministry. Work long hours, write good letters, call your county, city, and state government, and tell them of the need for your services. Do whatever it takes, and then pray and pray again. The final result is in God's hands.

I've tried in this chapter to give you some real nuts and bolts stuff, information that will help keep you out of trouble. There is also something very important to remember. If you make false statements and mail them in the form of a letter through the U.S. Postal Service, you could be convicted of mail fraud. Sometimes all of us can get carried away in the heat of the moment, but if you are guilty of this in conversation, make sure you don't get carried away through the U.S. mail.

Chapter Eight

To Ask or Not to Ask

There are definite standards in fundraising. Unfortunately, some people have no standards at all, and to some Christians any form of fundraising is sinful. I attended a church for some years where the belief was that as God is in charge, He'll supply everything you need, and so there's no need to ask. The assumption seemed to be that if you have to ask, then you're not in the will of God.

As the director of a new ministry or a ministry about to be, sooner or later you will run across pastors and people in the pews who hold to this assumption. You need to know how to deal with it, so here goes.

If a pastor of a church tells you that you're out of the will of God in asking for money, let him know that while you appreciate his position, it is one you don't necessarily agree with. Make him aware (courteously) that while you are glad that his needs are apparently met, there is a great difference between a church and a para-church ministry. Remind him that people have a biblical obligation to give to their church (a 10 percent tithe) and that while they also have an obligation to give offerings, many don't and that for those who do, there's no telling to whom they'll give them. Reassure him that you are not talking about begging, or psychological manipulation, but just presenting the facts plainly and letting the (potential) donor make up his or her mind.

There have been lots of examples recently of people who have abused the privilege of asking. I believe they have taken advantage of their donors' trust. When people act like that, it makes life harder for everyone.

Never, never, never stoop to "you pay, and I'll pray" tactics, employed by a few prominent television evangelists. If you do, I think you may deserve to close.

How Do You Ask?

As you've probably gathered by now, I have no problems at all with asking; it's HOW you ask.

The following is a reprint of an article by Russ Reid, the chairman of a large marketing company. It was printed in the *Rescue Magazine*, published by the International Union of Gospel Missions.

> What does it mean to have a faith ministry? Does it mean that your role is simply to pray and let God provide?
>
> Or, do you show that faith by actively seeking resources to fund the vision God has given you?
>
> This is a critical issue in raising funds for ministry, but it isn't new. Two of the most important leaders in Christian ministry–D.L. Moody and George Mueller–were good friends on opposite sides of the debate.
>
> Moody's attitude was that the Lord owned the cattle on a thousand hills, and all resources belonged to Him. He saw it as his challenge and opportunity to ask giants of industry to share their resources in Kingdom building. He chided his friend Mueller, however, for always explaining to potential supporters that he would not ask them for money, since God would supply all of his needs.
>
> Moody insisted, "By telling them you're not asking for money, you're *asking* for money. And of course, he was right.
>
> The interesting thing is that Mueller's orphanage, although a very important ministry in its day, has since closed its doors. On the other hand, D.L. Moody began a ministry that has outlived him by over 100 years.

Literally millions of people around the world hear the Gospel today because of the financial foundation that he built to launch and sustain his ministries.

It seems to me that Scripture is very clear that the type of active fundraising demonstrated by Dwight L. Moody has been a part of the work of God's people from Old Testament times through the development of the Christian church in the first century.

In Exodus 25, for example, God tells Moses to launch a "Capital Campaign" to build the Tabernacle. Moses is instructed to "Speak unto the children of Israel, that they bring Me an offering."

When it was time for the wall in Jerusalem to be rebuilt, Nehemiah solicited a major gift from the king of Babylon. "And the king granted me," the prophet wrote, "according to the good hand of my God."

Jesus' own ministry was financially supported by many disciples who gave financial contributions "out of their means." (Luke 8:3)

But it's the Apostle Paul who outlines biblical fundraising principles most clearly. Burning with enthusiasm to build new churches, he initiates a New Testament pledge plan: "Each one of you should set aside a sum of money in keeping with his income." (1 Cor. 16:1)

Paul also writes two chapters, II Corinthians 8 and 9, which are filled with tips for fundraisers. He not only uses all his persuasive powers to make the new church members enthusiastic givers, but he heaps praise and recognition on them for their previous generosity.

Paul also understands the importance of follow-up. "I thought it necessary," he explains to the Corinthians, "to urge the brothers to visit you in advance and finish the arrangements for the generous gift you promised." (2 Cor. 9:5)

The Bible is certainly not silent on the fact that all we have comes from God, and that our task is to challenge people with the opportunity to have significance in their lives by giving their resources to God.

So the real question is the most effective way to get that message out.

In today's world, technology has provided exciting new opportunities to find the thousands of people who may want to be a part of your ministry. Using new computer techniques, however, worries those who see technology as "worldly."

In fact, any kind of technology can raise this kind of anxiety. Some of you are old enough to remember when evangelists repudiated and denounced radio as an instrument of the devil, only to have them change their mind and see its potential to be a vehicle to tell the world of the saving love of Jesus.

Not many of us would discredit or disallow the work of a CPA to do an audit on our books, or an attorney to help us sort out the ramifications of a property purchase. Or in more recent times, to accept the help of a computer in making information available to us.

Should we be any less hesitant to utilize space advertising, direct mail, television, planned giving and major gift campaigns to provide the resources to fund all that God has called us to do? I think not.

Does this mean that trusting God is unnecessary? Of course not. Rich or poor, we have to trust God for every breath we take. But there are some clear distinctions between which responsibilities are God's and which belong to us.

I'm often reminded of that when people ask me "Isn't it a miracle that thousands of people always come to Billy Graham's crusades?"

I have to say "No. That isn't a miracle. Billy Graham's organization uses every resource available to ensure there will be a crowd."

The miracle happens at the invitation, when thousands walk the aisle to profess Christ as Lord.

In the same way, when money is raised for your mission, it takes hard work and solid know-how in the field of fundraising.

> That isn't the miracle. But after you have in faith spent the money to reach out to people in need, God begins to transform their lives. That is the miracle.
>
> I believe that rescue mission work deserves the kind of funding base that will allow each of you to do more of what God is calling you to do.
>
> Isn't it time we set aside forever the idea that being a faith ministry requires us to ignore resources which can help us reach more people more effectively? (Reprinted by permission.)

I totally endorse what Russ Reid writes. He is an experienced professional fundraiser, who has helped raise hundreds of thousands and possibly millions of dollars for missions around the United States.

Now if all forms of marketing and asking are wrong for you and you consider them sin, then you need to obey God, and pray. But I have to say that I don't honestly expect your shelter to get very far, or last very long, if that's the route you take.

The typical attrition rate for a mailing list is 20 percent each year. That means it will only take you five years to lose your entire donor base. Speaking from a shelter operator's vantage point, there's something about being in the shelter business that tends to keep your feet on the ground. Maybe it's because we, as shelter operators, have to deal with such "earthly" or "worldly" needs as well as spiritual needs.

To balance this out a little, I'm reminded of something that I heard someone say a few years ago. The person said he usually has to tell Christians not to be so heavenly minded that they're no earthly good. He said that conversely with shelter operators, he has to remind them that God still works miracles. Keep this in mind as you ponder what has been said in this chapter. I don't want to give you the idea that God doesn't work miracles. He does. I want to make sure you know that just as God still heals supernaturally today but also uses doctors, God still provides supernaturally for homeless shelters and other para-church ministries today, but He also uses mailing lists, marketing directors, and the latest in electronic gadgetry.

As to whether you should use a Christian or secular company, you and your board will need to seek the wisdom of the Lord on that. But let me ask you a question. If you suddenly discovered that you had terminal cancer, but there was a chance of your life being saved by new technological advances and some special form of new surgery, I'm sure you would want to avail yourself of that opportunity. If you had the choice of two surgeons, one who was Christian and a second-rate surgeon, and the other who was an atheist but a first-rate surgeon, what would you do? I hope that you would (and I think that you would) choose the first-rate surgeon and pray for his salvation.

When you go out to eat, do you ask for a Christian waiter? When you go to get your hair cut, do you ask for a Christian hairdresser? Probably not. So as you consider which sort of marketing company to select, pray. Then get with your board and your spiritual advisors. Don't ask your potential marketing company if they're Christians. Ask them for a list of their clients. Ask for permission to call them and get some sort of reference. Ask the company for references on in-town work as well as out-of-town jobs. You're considering a big investment.

Joy Junction recently undertook a large acquisition mailing. By the time we had finished, we (through our marketing company) had mailed out about 185,000 pieces. The job cost us a considerable amount of money, plus a lot more in postage. (And the postage was using the cheapest form of bulk rate postage available.) A lot of money went into that mailing, but there's no shelter around (Remember the statistics I just gave you about the 20 percent a year attrition rate from your donor base.) that can afford not to do an acquisition mailing. If you don't, someone else will. And Christian or not, they'll end up stealing donors who very possibly would have been willing to help finance your vision.

Before you think that spending such a large amount of money is totally ridiculous, wait a moment. Joy Junction anticipates gaining thousands of dollars from the acquisition mailing and three thousand *new* donors. Think what the additional revenue from three thousand new donors could do for your mission!

As Russ Reid pointed out, there are tremendous skills involved in marketing. It's not just writing the letter and mailing it out, there's also the selection of the specialized areas of town to send it to. It is adequately keeping track of the responses, as well as a large number of other variables.

As I have pointed out in another chapter, there's a good chance that you might have to do your own marketing for a while. If there's no way you can afford a professional marketing company, consider finding one, explaining your plight, and asking them for some helpful insight and advice. I would also be glad to help you.

To ask or not to ask? I believe the answer is *ask*–just don't beg.

[illegible]

[illegible]

[illegible] might have [illegible]

[illegible]

Chapter Nine

We're Here, Folks

You can have a great shelter for the homeless, a great alcohol and drug rehab, or meal-feeding site, but if you don't let the community know you're out there, it won't do you any good. All you'll have is a lot of empty beds.

Even as I was preparing to open Joy Junction in 1986, I got on the telephone and called various agencies, "Hi, I'm Jeremy Reynalds, and I'm about to open a brand new shelter for homeless and abused women and homeless families. Take the number down, and if there's anyway I can help you, feel free to give me a call." And call they did. Joy Junction began to shelter families even before our announced opening date. From that point on, I stayed on the telephone and still spend an enormous amount of time on the telephone today.

I always make a point of cultivating relationships with agency workers I meet. You can have a great ministry, but if another agency representative has a bad experience with one of your staff, that person will think badly about your agency. There's a great danger of that one bad experience overriding all the other positive things happening at your agency.

About every three months, I have my secretary write to all the area agencies reminding them that we're still here, and we want to help them. Social service and other similar work is very high-stress and in many cases has a high-staff turnover. You have to remind new workers of your presence and desire to cultivate a relationship with them. At least initially, people are much more likely to refer clients to your agency if they have a specific person to call.

Call all the churches in town and tell them about the service you offer. Many shelters refer to themselves as an "arm of the church," but this term could apply to every para-church ministry. Most pastors are very busy people who don't have adequate time to take care of their own flock without trying to screen the needs of the homeless as well. They'll welcome a call to tell them that they have someone to whom they can turn anytime. (Such conversations might also lead to inclusion in the church's budget at some point down the road!)

Let the community service clubs know you're there and are willing to come speak (at a moment's notice) about your organization. Groups like the Kiwanis, Civitans, and Rotary are always looking for speakers, and if you let them know you're there, as well as giving them the freedom to call you at a moment's notice, I can almost guarantee you'll get some takers.

The Media (Yes, Really!)

You're also going to have to work with the press. Yes, the press! I know some Christians have a conspiratorial attitude about the press, but with prayer and God's blessing, the press can go to work for you.

Here are some guidelines for communicating with the media.

You need to know what information to send to the media. There's a good chance that if it's something you would be interested in reading, it's news. Examples include new staff or staff promotions, additional services you're offering to your clients, or a new location, building, or project. Other examples include the receipt of a large donation or a human interest story that your shelter finds itself in the middle of.

Also, help the media. If you send public service announcements, tell the station how many seconds your announcement runs. If you're sending a press release, keep it short and to the point. Make sure the thrust of what you want to say is communicated in the first sentence. Busy editors don't have the time to wade through a whole lot of information to get to what they need. Less is best!

Know when to send and when not to send. In other words, try and get some sense of what is newsworthy and what isn't. You might even consider enrolling in some basic journalism courses at your local university or community college. It won't do anything except help you in your ability to relate to the media. Don't forget to present all the information about your agency to the media in a short and timely fashion. (It'll help you get their respect, as well as save you excessive typing and eyestrain!)

Please, please, please, don't "evangelically embellish" to make you look better. Make sure everything you send the media is accurate–the media doesn't want to publish errors. If you have to use quotes, make sure you attribute (say who said what). The media doesn't want to spend time checking. The more time the media has to spend on your story/announcement, unless it's a really hot news item, the less chance there is of it being published or read. Always include a call back number for the media. If they're working under great pressure the day they deal with your story, the more time you can save them the better.

Baby the media. No, I don't say that to sound facetious. I really mean it. Let me explain.

As well as running Joy Junction, I am also a journalism student at the University of New Mexico. While covering then vice-presidential candidate Al Gore's visit to Albuquerque, I was very impressed with the way campaign organizers went out of their way to help the press. The media was provided a complete text of Gore's speech as well as a complete schedule of his upcoming activities. Anything the press wanted they appeared to get.

Picture how a busy reporter feels, especially if he's struggling to make accurate notes of what could be a complex and technical speech. What a difference it makes to have a complete copy of the text handed to him. He can listen to the speech, enjoy, and assimilate it, all the time knowing that he has a copy of the complete text at his fingertips. During the last election, the Democrats took care of the press, and it paid off.

What I'm going to tell you next you may not like, and that's OK. But if you want to succeed in your relationship with the press and maintain a healthy, ongoing relationship with them, you need to remember and do what I'm going to tell you. It's so simple, but absolutely essential.

Be available to the media twenty-four-hours a day, seven days a week. Give the media every telephone number, beeper, mobile, or fax number that you have. Always be polite, respectful, and glad when the media calls you. *Never make yourself unavailable to the media.* No matter what time a reporter calls you, answer his or her question truthfully and briefly. Remember that the media needs quotes and information when they need it. Their time schedule might not necessarily fit in with yours, so get whatever equipment you need to make sure you're always accessible.

Make sure that your staff knows who's allowed to talk to the press. If you're the only one, inform the staff that they must call you if the press shows up unannounced.

Be scrupulously honest with the press. Reporters are trained to "sniff out" things that you might want to keep hidden. If the press asks you about a problem, don't pretend that it doesn't exist or you don't know anything about it. Obviously give your side of the story, but be honest and accept blame. Remember that if there's a problem, even if you aren't necessarily responsible, if you're the head of the organization, the buck stops with you, and you ultimately shoulder at least some of the blame.

Dealing with the Media in a Crisis

The Albuquerque Journal printed a great article by staff writer Paul Legau about how companies can deal with the media in a crisis, and I'm reprinting it for you.

> Whether Americans like to admit it or not, they are interested and titillated by the coverage of crises by the nation's media.

That's why "60 Minutes" and "20-20" are popular television shows, according to a management-crisis expert. They satisfy the public's voyeuristic side, he said, except when the crisis is in your own business.

"God gave us two ends," said Marvin "Swede" Johnson, "one to sit on and one to think with. Success in a crisis situation depends upon which end you use the most."

Johnson is Coors Brewing Company's vice president for corporate affairs. Before joining the Golden, Colorado-based firm, Johnson served as the University of New Mexico's administrative vice-president for student affairs.

With each organization, Johnson helped in handling potentially disastrous situations–the Coors mouse-in-a-can controversy, and Lobogate, UNM's basketball scandal.

Although most national media coverage involves crises at larger companies, Johnson said New Mexico small businesses are just as susceptible to a crisis and the aftermath–media scrutiny.

Johnson recently told an audience of business and community leaders "how to handle the media during a crisis" and how to avoid responding to the press "with throat-clearing, stammering gibberish."

The media drive a crisis, Johnson said. "If they don't like you, they can prolong coverage of your disaster an interminable, excruciatingly long time. They make the difference in what kind of image is presented to the public."

Johnson used the example of how United Airlines handled the cartwheeling crash-landing of one of its aircraft at Sioux City, Iowa, three years ago. The fiery crash killed 111 of the jet's 296 passengers.

However, the story wasn't about the mechanical defects that caused the plane's hydraulic system to fail, said Johnson, but rather the heroic flying ability of Al Haynes, the jetliner's captain.

The media reported the event as the story of a corporate hero, not a corporate mistake, he said.

"Much of this had to do with the way United's communications people handled the press immediately following the crash," Johnson said.

Every business faces a multitude of disaster possibilities, he said, including fires, accidents, market shifts, product failures and environmental problems.

Johnson said that Coors has an issues-management team that monitors potential crises, such as responding to a reporter who calls and says: "We'd like to know why one of your consumers in Florida found a mouse in a can of Coors beer?"

Johnson said Coors was fully exonerated in the "mouse crisis of 1988." The person who put the mouse in the can went to jail.

However, the controversy surrounding the mouse "turned into a three-month media circus complete with law suits, declining sales and falling consumer confidence in our product," said Johnson.

In the mouse case, Coors had several short-term, and long-term problems–determining how the rodent got into the can and turning around the lack of consumer confidence, he said.

Once the problem is identified, businesses should conduct their best case, he said. *No matter how terrible the event, a company still has its own story to tell the media.*

Johnson said a crisis-management plan should contain favorable, pertinent facts about the business to guarantee a quick response to media questions. He used a hypothetical example–prior to the company's mishap, it had not lost one hour of work in the last five years.

"I know most small-business people barely have time to manage employees, seek new customers and keep the old ones happy," said Johnson, "let alone put together a crisis plan that lists important facts about the organization."

If a small business can't compile information ahead of time, he said, the owner must spend a few minutes pulling it together when the crisis occurs, because it makes telling the company's side of the story much easier.

Taking some ideas from former American Motors chairman Gerald Meyers' book, "When It Hits the Fan," Johnson suggested the following steps in managing any crisis:

The business owner or manager should let everybody inside the organization know you are in charge of handling media inquiries.

Pinpoint the problem.

Construct your best case. Tell your own story about the crisis.

Accommodate the media. Develop a rapport with the journalists covering the event. Tell the whole story and get it over with quickly to minimize the length of time that headlines stay on the front page.

Be honest and ethical. In this way, you won't have to worry about being caught in lies, which will be discovered anyway.

Speak with a clear voice–avoiding industry jargon or double speak.

Be available 24 hours a day–reporters want information when they want information.

Consider telling your story through advertising as well.

Demonstrate your company's concerns, showing real human information.

In his seminars, Dr. Martin Stoler, a crisis-communication consultant, uses the case of the Exxon-Valdez oil spill to demonstrate the importance of a company in crisis showing concern, Johnson said.

Johnson asked those attending the luncheon the same thing Stoler asks his audiences: "How long was it before Lawrence Rawl, Exon's chief executive officer, went to Alaska after the oil tanker hit the reef?

A week maybe?" Johnson asked, "A month? No, it was one year before Rawl made the trip to the site of the spill because he was trying to distance himself from the event."

Johnson said Rawl should have met the problem head-on–flown to Alaska, knelt on the beach and picked up an oil-soaked duck, held it up to the news cameras and said: "This is a tragedy of major proportions. I will not rest until this situation is rectified."

If a corporate executive demonstrates legitimate concern, Johnson said, he or she eliminates the justification for the press constantly being on the company's case.

Johnson listed the following no-no's when a company in crisis deals with the media:

Don't speculate publicly about what you don't know.

Don't minimize the problem to the press. If it's serious, the media will find out.

Don't let the story dribble out, because each new fact will bring a new headline.

Don't blame anyone for anything.

Don't play favorites among television, radio and print reporters. Media rivalry is alive and well without your influence.

Don't say "no comment"–it makes you look guilty.

"When have you ever believed the innocence of a person who sits across from Mike Wallace (of "60 minutes") and says 'No comment?' Johnson asked.

"Instead, explain why you can't–that you are still investigating the problem, for example; or, that a lawsuit is pending."

Johnson recommends one final step after the crisis subsides–follow up. The head of a company should ask himself or herself: "Where are we now, and where do we have to go from here?" (*The Albuquerque Journal*, 1992. Used by permission.)

Yes, the article does apply to you. Memorize it because it contains advice that could save your ministry in a time of crisis.

Dealing with a Crisis

Remember that despite your best efforts, shelter ministry can be very crisis-prone.

There have been times when I've left the shelter, and it was in an absolutely peaceful state. You wouldn't think that anyone had a care in the world, and then a few minutes later, my beeper starts vibrating, and it's my staff asking how to handle a crisis that's sprung up without any warning.

Here's an example of a "crisis" that could only happen within a homeless shelter. I firmly think that it was averted because of my good relationship with the press and many of the other agencies in town.

It started off like any other Friday–letters to write, the phone to answer, and general run-of-the-mill business to attend to. Then my secretary came in with a worried look on her face.

"Jeremy, it's [name omitted] and he says he's got to speak to you immediately. It's urgent."

"Hello, this is Jeremy."

"Yeah, Jeremy. What's going on at the shelter? You guys serving rotten water?"

"What?!"

The amazing conversation continued.

"We just had this couple down here complaining about your water. They brought this vial of water that has stuff that looks like toilet paper floating in it, and the water's yellow. They're saying that this is the sort of water that you're serving at the shelter, and this is a sample out of the bathroom. Oh, and they're also saying that they got TB at the shelter. Don't want to scare you, but I just thought you should know."

The man wished me a good day (ha!) and hung up. I quickly ascertained the situation.

It's been standard procedure for awhile now when people being referred to Joy Junction don't want to stay at the shelter, they either drive around town for awhile and call the person back and say we're full, or they vilify the shelter in some way. This was obviously a prime case of the latter!

Even though this wasn't the best way to start the day, at that early time of the morning I still didn't have any idea of what a day it was going to be!

Crisis and Vacation?!

Some weeks prior I had scheduled a couple of days out of town with my wife and family. We were to stay with some friends in El Paso. I didn't feel comfortable telling my wife and kids that the whole trip was off because one of our guests had a grudge against us. (Doing that might be a quick way of encouraging your wife to mount a grudge against you!)

So we took off, and I thought I was gradually beginning to unwind and enjoy myself. Then about one hundred or so miles south of Albuquerque, I felt that familiar vibration on my hip that meant someone was trying to reach me on my beeper. I looked and read a message from my answering service to call a local motel.

Grabbing my cellular phone with some resignation, I dialed the number. The clerk said she felt she should call me; there was some bad things being said about the shelter, and she wanted to make sure I was aware of everything that was going on.

"Jeremy, this is what's been happening. I just got a call from a clerk at another motel who's a good friend of mine. She told me that there are some people running around the city who claim to have TB, and they're saying they got it from dirty water at your facility. Those same people just called me as well and asked for a free room. I know you and the work you do, and didn't believe it, but thought I should call you."

I thanked my kind informant and filled her in on what I thought was happening.

"Those people want a motel room, and what's evolved in Albuquerque with Joy Junction being the only shelter is that everyone gets referred to us, so if they don't want to stay at Joy Junction and don't have a legitimate reason, they have a real problem.

"I think they dredged the potty for urine, put some toilet paper in it, took it down to a local agency, and said, 'Look!

This is the sort of stuff that Joy Junction's doing. They're unsanitary, so don't send us there. In fact, we've been there and we've gotten TB.'"

The clerk understood the situation very well, which made things at least a little bit easier.

I figured I should call some of the other Albuquerque agencies to see who else had heard about our special brand of water. Calling around a number of agencies I found that a bunch had, but one or two smart ones had already taken steps to defuse the situation and said, "Look! That stuff about Joy Junction needs to stop immediately, and anyone who wants to keep on with it can see me and spend the night elsewhere."

Don't forget that while all this was happening, I was in the van with my wife and children headed for a happy weekend's break in El Paso. I can't quite remember the look on my wife's face while all this was going on, but I seem to recall that it was less than happy–maybe more like, "I've been through all this before."

I called the shelter's operations manager and alerted him to what was going on and told all the staff to notify me immediately if any media should happen to call. I didn't think they would run with one side of the story without talking to me first, but there was always that possibility . . .

Meanwhile I was also asking myself if I should call the media and inform them about the situation, or if to do so could draw unnecessary attention to something that might resolve itself. As we were getting closer to El Paso, I decided not to do anything for that night and to call a few stations in the morning.

Whether or not to call the media in the hope of fending off a potential crisis will depend on your particular situation. If you've established a good rapport with the press, and they know you're for real and you really do what you say you do, then it might not be a bad idea to call them.

However, if you're still brand new or you've gotten off to a rocky start with the media, then it might be a good idea to leave things well alone and pray that the media doesn't hear about what's going on. But if they do, then respond promptly, courteously, and absolutely truthfully. As the writer of the article above says, in the end the media will always find out.

So Saturday morning I called the television stations and told them what was going on. They weren't overly concerned, which I believe was a reflection of the relationship of trust and honesty I've built up with the assignment editors at these stations.

I reported to the press what I had found when I called the chemist who tests our water monthly (We operate from a well.) the day before. We had taken him five samples to test.

Upon returning to Albuquerque I called the state environmental health department and asked them to send their man down to take another four samples. He had already been alerted. If you don't know how fast gossip and rumor travels in homeless circles, you'll find out very soon!

The furor began to die down when I received the second set of test results from our chemist. All the water samples were clean, as I had expected. A few days after that, the state notified me with the same results. I called the *Albuquerque Journal* and asked them if they would publish something to say that Joy Junction's water is clean and healthy. They agreed to if I would send them the test results from the state and the chemist.

Me—Have a Crisis?

I guess the lesson is this. Anyone can have a crisis. As you've learned in this chapter, how you handle it will play a major part in determining how the media will handle it. In handling the water situation, I drew upon years of honest dealings with Albuquerque's media. Still, seven years of honesty with the media followed by just one incident of dishonesty or being less than forthcoming will hurt you for many years to come.

Build relationships with the press, don't try to pull any of the stunts that I've seen some Christian ministries play (Oh, I don't have to have my water tested because I'm a Christian!) and be available and honest. Above all, pray, pray, and keep on praying whenever you talk to the press. You have an agenda (doing the Lord's work, feeding and sheltering, etc.), and the press has an agenda (a story). If the two agendas are going to successfully gel over the long haul, you need the Lord's blessing and favor.

Chapter Ten

Opening Day

It's opening day. You should be excited, as this day is the culmination of months of prayer, strategizing, and planning. Finally, your vision has become a reality, and the long-awaited ministry is open.

When I opened Joy Junction in 1986, I had spent long hours on the phone calling around to various Albuquerque social service agencies telling them that Joy Junction would be open soon. This did a couple of very important things. The other agencies heard about the opening of the shelter from me and not from someone else. Hearing something directly from the person concerned is one of the best ways to fight off any fear and the resulting gossip.

Secondarily, it was a way of spreading around town the word about us and giving other agencies the opportunity to refer to us if they so wished.

A few days before opening day, Joy Junction received its first family.

The man had just been released from prison and was on parole. Along with him were his wife and two children. I was happy. Joy Junction was off and running!

I had received a call from adult probation and parole. Somehow they had heard about our upcoming opening and wondered if we might be willing to admit a family even prior to opening day. I consented on condition that the family indicated a willingness to help out with building cleanup. The parole officer said the only way that this gentleman could get out of prison was if he had the offer of a place to stay from a shelter like ours. So the family came, and the same day or thereabouts, another family called. We had families, and we weren't even open! What a way to begin!

The time passed, and I was kept busy answering phones, making sure the evening meal was cooked, and teaching the evening Bible study. Everyday, before I knew it, it was very late, and my wife called me to ask if I planned to come home.

An article by staff writer David Morrissey appeared in the September 1986 *Albuquerque Journal* a couple of days after we opened, and it was the start of what was to be a very fruitful relationship with all of the Albuquerque media. Here's some of it.

> The Friday dedication of the Joy Junction emergency shelter underscores one of Albuquerque's contradictions–in the midst of a citywide housing boom, a growing number of people have no place to live.
>
> The Department of Housing and Urban development says more than 8,000 housing units were built during the last two years in Albuquerque. Another 2,000 units are now under construction.
>
> There are so many apartments in the city, 15 percent are vacant–a rate twice the national average. At the same time, there are many with no place to call home.
>
> Workers at Albuquerque missions and emergency shelters say the need is growing.
>
> A potluck supper at 6 p.m. Friday will show off one effort to meet the needs of the homeless, said the Rev. Jeremy Reynalds, director of the shelter.
>
> Scheduled to open Oct. 1 [1986], the facility at 4500 2nd St. SW, is located at what was the dormitory of the now-closed Our Lady of Lourdes High School.
>
> The building, owned by DARE, Drug Alcohol Rehabilitation Enterprises, has been leased to serve as a shelter, said Reynalds.

> Joy Junction will provide both emergency and long-term shelter for single women and families, Reynalds said. The need for shelter for these people in Albuquerque is greatest, he added.
>
> Prior to the opening of Joy Junction, which will be able to house a maximum of seven families and 10 women, there were only three emergency shelters in the city with facilities to house families. Those shelters, serving Albuquerque's metropolitan area of more than 400,000 people, could handle a maximum of 14 families.
>
> Joy Junction, a non-denominational ministry as well as a shelter, will be funded by donations, Reynalds said. It will not seek or accept federal, state or city funds. The shelter especially needs food and bedding, he said.
>
> Reynalds said he expects the shelter to help out those who are "temporarily economically disadvantaged"—people who can be helped to find new jobs and housing.
>
> Because of the current economic climate, there are people using shelters today who never imagined they would need emergency housing, Reynalds said. (Used by permission.)

Who Am I?

The first month passed quickly, and sometimes I wondered who and possibly what I was. I was literally doing everything for the first month or so. I was the executive director and the administrator of the whole shelter. I was also "hustling" the food to make sure that there was always some food of some sort in-house. I answered the phone and typed all of my own letters. On top of that, I prepared the evening Bible studies and occasionally left to go home to my own wife and family.

So who are you? The answer is that all you can be is you—someone very ordinary but still very special because you are obeying God's calling on your life. You have been chosen by God to fulfill a very special function.

The reality is that like the Apostle Paul you need to be all things to all people that, by so being, some might come to a saving knowledge of the Lord Jesus Christ.

You need to be very wise and discerning and recognize that you are not necessarily called to preach the gospel to everyone. Everyone is called to hear the gospel, but you might not be the one who is charged with the responsibility of delivering that message. Thus, you do not have to tell every homeless person, the mayor, the city council, and every city, county, and state official whom you encounter about Jesus.

To some people you will be an administrator, to some people you will be an agency head, to some people you will be a minister and a pastor. You have literally been given the opportunity to be all things to all men, and don't forget that you have to earn the right to preach the gospel to people.

As you launch forth on this exciting new venture, pastors, business people, your donors, vendors, and a whole variety of other people in the community will be watching you very carefully to see how you conduct yourself. For example, do you pay your bills on time? And if not, do you adequately communicate with people to whom you owe money to let them know what's going on? To be able to preach the gospel to people, you have to operate in an upright and above-board manner. People will be watching you very carefully.

Have you also thought of what your emotional reaction will be when either you or some volunteers have labored long and hard to cook a good meal, warm, tasty, and nutritious—the sort of meal that you wouldn't hesitate to feed your own family—and you open up the serving hatches and hear a couple of guests look disparagingly at the food and say in a loud voice, "You know what? I wouldn't serve that to my dog!"

That's when you need to know that you're doing what you're doing for the Lord, and you will be and you will do whatever the Lord calls you to be and do. If you don't adopt this posture, you will become quickly disillusioned and easily hurt.

David Morrissey of *The Albuquerque Journal* wrote a another piece on us on 27 November 1986, shortly after we opened. This time, they featured one of our first families. Here is some of that article.

> Pilgrims at the first Thanksgiving gratefully thanked God for bringing them through a difficult and uncertain year.
>
> Ted and Judy Kotoff will offer much the same prayer as they sit down today for their Thanksgiving dinner in Albuquerque.
>
> The Kotoffs, both 32, are in many ways a typical family. They work hard, try to save their money and want the best for their four-year-old son Jesse.
>
> Thanksgiving is a day they reflect on their blessings.
>
> But this year Ted and Judy Kotoff are homeless.
>
> Their Thanksgiving table is at Joy Junction, an Albuquerque shelter for homeless families and single women, where they now live in one small bedroom.
>
> They arrived in Albuquerque three weeks ago from South Carolina. They lived in a trailer there–sometimes employed, sometimes looking for work. When jobs proved scarce, they headed west.
>
> It wasn't so much they intended to stop in Albuquerque, Ted Kotoff explained. It was just that here their meager savings ran out.
>
> By chance they heard of Joy Junction, a shelter in the dormitory of the now-closed Our Lady of Lourdes High School at 4500 Second SW, run by the Rev. Jeremy Reynalds.
>
> "We called Jeremy and he took us in," said Ted. "It's been like an oasis in the storm."
>
> "We're both painters," said Judy Kotoff, adding that she was also an electronics technician while Ted had worked as a mechanic and a musician. "We want to work. We're not afraid of hard work."
>
> They followed the construction jobs in South Carolina and other states, trying to make enough to settle down, Ted said. But work was infrequent. Stories of high-

paying jobs the next state over proved to be wistful thinking.

When construction went bust, the Kotoffs got on with a carnival in South Carolina, operating rides. But when the carnival operator failed to pay them wages they thought they had earned, they decided to make a new start.

In Albuquerque they found temporary jobs as telephone solicitors, earning $4 an hour, 20 hours week. While staying at Joy Junction, they hope to save enough for an apartment, and find better-paying job . . . .

While the homeless are difficult to count and categorize, the federal Department of Housing and Urban Development says they fall into three categories: people with chronic alcohol and drug problems, people with personal crises, such as battered women and runaway children, and people who have suffered severe economic setbacks, such as losing a job.

City officials across the nation report an increase in the number of middle-class Americans forced into emergency shelters through job loss or sudden catastrophic expenses.

Many of these new poor "are just like you and me," Reynalds said. "They're not street people, but people temporarily down on their luck."

Ted and Judy Kotoff are thankful today, but they aren't satisfied.

If they have their way, the nation's homeless population will be cut by at least one family.

Little Foxes

I remember coming to the end of our first month; there were a lot of things on my mind. We had some discontented guests and some discontented donors. After having run a shelter in Santa Fe for four years, I sort of expected both but hadn't thought that the discontent would manifest itself this quickly.

I'm going to spend some time on what at first might appear to be some very small and insignificant things, but it's those "little" things that can cause the shelter operator, or any head of any para-church ministry, much grief. The same thing would apply to any other people ministry the Lord might be leading you to start.

First, I want to reiterate some previously mentioned items which are very important. Do not open a shelter for homeless people (or don't get into any sort of ministry) expecting the homeless–or your clients, parishioners, or guests–to be grateful. Some may be but most won't be. Do what you do as unto the Lord.

Try and empathize with those you're dealing with and their situation. Homeless people and drug addicts are going through one of the worst experiences they've ever had in their lives. They don't want to stay in a shelter–and probably not in a rehab either–and in all likelihood, anything that goes wrong is going to be blamed on you and not their own inadequacies.

Look to the Lord for thanks and Him only. He will stop you from getting burned out. There was an Associated Press article by David Briggs I read recently that reminds me about this. I think it is well worth passing on. Here it is.

> Psychologists, in an effort to determine why some people are exceptionally caring, have studied members of religious orders and found the quality separating members who enjoyed caring for the poorest of the poor, from those who responded out of duty, was the depth of their personal relationship with God.
>
> The findings by David McClelland and Carol Franz of Boston University go beyond traditional psychological theories that individuals essentially help others out of self interest–whether to fulfill a personal desire to aid others or reduce the guilt felt for walking by someone in need.
>
> "For helpful people there is a third force in the transaction, namely what might be most generally called a 'benevolent authority.' For these religious (people) the third force is more simply God," the researchers said.
>
> The caring-people study was part of a larger study on "The Future of Religious Orders in the United States," funded by the Lilly Endowment.

McClelland, a professor emeritus of psychology at Harvard University who is renowned for his work in motivational psychology, and Franz studied 54 members of religious orders. One group contained 30 people regarded in their communities as exceptionally caring. The second group included 24 members identified as typical by their communities, but who would still be generally considered as helpful and caring.

In general, those in the "caring religious" group were more joyful in their work, were more likely to establish personal relationships with the people they helped, and were more likely to describe activities such as visiting the sick and helping the poor as being very valuable.

Why do helpful people help? The researchers found that in the words of the old hymn, where charity and love prevail there God is ever found.

Asked to describe a healing experience, four times as many caring religious mentioned God in the experience. Members of the caring group also frequently described contemplative prayer as being very valuable.

Relying on God produced some practical benefits, the researchers found.

For starters, caring religious do not as easily burn out since they do not consider themselves responsible for doing the healing. They are also less likely to be manipulative as caregivers, because they believe that it is God, and not them, that is the source of the healing.

"They don't see it as coming from themselves. They see themselves as coming from and identified with something larger than themselves," McClelland said.

Sharing their relationship with God is more important than fixing the immediate needs of the individual.

"They don't stress the suffering and need . . . nearly as much as those who have socialized power motives," McClelland said.

Take Mother Teresa as an example, McClelland said. The reason she can describe the joy in picking worms off a homeless man who will die a few hours later is "because this is the way she identifies with Jesus and the way he would want it."

In the act of seeing God in the people they serve, all of the filters of class, race and status that many people bring to relationships tend to disappear, said the Rev. David Nygren, who coordinated the larger study on religious orders with Sister Miriam Ukeritis.

"They pass through a barrier most of us have based on our own human needs," Nygren said.

The introduction of God may shatter traditional assumptions about why people help, but one scholar said the findings are reasonable.

"I think by all means it makes very good sense," said Wayne Rollins of Assumption College, chairman of the consultation on psychology and biblical studies for the Society of Biblical Literature.

"I think that altruism which is rooted in a broader sense of self is a native potential for all human beings," he said.

Outside of religion, the implications of the research may even extend to superb physicians and judges for whom the higher power outside oneself can be simply medicine or the law, McClelland said.

"No matter what you do, if you're a chairwoman or an investment banker, your relationships are less self-centered . . . and your relationships are naturally better," McClelland said. (Used by permission.)

Hazards of the Job

Also, learn very quickly that as a homeless shelter operator, a caregiver–whether you're dealing with the homeless, or dysfunctional people in any shape, form, or variety–in dealing with your clients and your donors, you have to work with two entirely different sets of expectations.

Take cleanliness of the facility grounds as a choice example. As the agency grows, there's no way that you'll be able to provide cleanup for all the people staying at the facility. You shouldn't have to. You will have to implement a chore system, and you'll have to check up on residents after they've completed their chore duties. To many dysfunctional people, it's quite natural to leave a trail of messes after them. If the dumpster is overflowing and you say empty it, you mean empty it now. It also has to be emptied with good reason. A full or overflowing dumpster is an eyesore as well as a health hazard. So you tell a particular resident to clean up around the dumpster.

You've had a long day already and guess what. This time you don't check on the resident to make sure that he or she has completed the task. They do a sloppy job, and everything is a mess. Donors come down and don't complain to you. They just start talking around town, "That place is always dirty."

To add insult to injury, the same donors bring some food down, and walking in the door, they see what they think are lazy residents "sitting around." Again, you don't hear about it first hand. The "showdown" comes many months later. You've been invited to speak for a group, and after you make your presentation, there's time for a question and answer session.

Someone stands up and in a sarcastic voice says, "Oh, I thought that you had a work ethic or some sort of work policy."

You reassure her that you do and ask her specifically what she means.

She says, "Oh, when a group of us came down a few weeks ago we brought down a lot of food from a drive that the club had." She tells you in graphic terms how heavy the cans were and how hard the group had worked. And then the punch:

"Well, we walked through the door and there were all those people just sitting around. I really resent that. They can't help?"

You try to explain to her some of the dynamics of running a helping agency–facts like "clinical depression," not a copout, but depression so bad that it can physically immobilize someone. You tell her about the increasing number of mentally ill people whom the shelter is being asked to take care of, people who look normal, but who are totally dysfunctional. You go on to talk about the people working the nightshift who just want to hang out before resting. You try to tell her how being homeless is a demoralizing and, to some extent, dehumanizing ego-stripping experience, but all your efforts are to no avail.

So you conclude and say no more. To say more would be inappropriate and quite possibly lead to an argument.

Why Do So Few People Understand?

How do you handle stuff like that? Incidents like the one I've described happen everyday in shelters, drug rehabs, and crisis pregnancy centers all across the United States.

You must realize that such gossip is an in-built peril of doing anything for the Lord. Those who *do* generally get criticized by those who *don't* do (but think they know all the answers). But then realizing that, you do all you can and leave the results in the Lord's hands, like the following.

You have to make sure that the grounds are kept as clean as possible. There will obviously be times when you fall short, and donors are angry, but just do the very best you can as unto the Lord and let Him take care of the rest.

Try and educate the community about homelessness, alcohol abuse, unplanned pregnancy, and so on. I've found that very few people are adequately informed about what being homeless actually does to you. Yes, in some cases, people have become homeless/alcoholic through making inappropriate choices, but in many cases they didn't become that way overnight, and they won't just "snap out of it" overnight either. Be informed. Let your donors know how it feels to be homeless, pregnant, unmarried, and so on.

Ask them (nicely) how they would feel if they had no kitchen to cook in. Ask them how they would feel if they had no job, and their next meal and night's shelter were dependent on someone else's charity (or lack of it).

About two o'clock one morning, the phone rang.

"Good morning, Joy Junction."

"This is the Sheriff's Department. We've just had a 911 call from the shelter, someone who claims that they've had stuff stolen. What's going on?"

The upshot of the story was that a mentally ill lady had called 911 from the public phone at the shelter to complain about the treatment she had received from a local hospital. She believed that the hospital had stolen her belongings and was keeping it from her in "an upper room" somewhere.

The police weren't too thrilled about being called out, but they came anyway. The woman wouldn't settle down, so the police ended up having to handcuff her and take her away.

Should we have tried to settle her down? Possibly. Would it have worked? Probably not. Did we like having to send her to a hopelessly overworked county mental health facility, knowing that in all probability she would be out on the streets in a few hours? No. But we had a responsibility to all the other residents to ensure them a good night's sleep, as well as to the sheriff's department to help prevent any more crank calls.

How do we handle all these stressful situations? By realizing that we're running a shelter for the Lord and that we can only do what we can with the resources which He allows us to have. We also have to commit all of our residents to the Lord, both past, present, and future. We must try to help them, as much as we can, to see that the Lord can do so much more, and that the destiny of all of our clients or parishioners ultimately lies in the Lord's hands.

Finding a Helping Hand

For sharing and networking and for getting some frustrating experiences off your chest, consider joining the International Union of Gospel Missions. The IUGM is a loose-knit association of rescue ministries that gathers together for conferences and fellowship and provides resource materials, etc. If it's not a shelter you're considering opening, then find out if there's a "trade group" for your ministry, like the Association of Christian Schools International.

It is also a necessity to have a supportive church and pastor where you fellowship on a regular basis. Last but not least, use your board as a resource. They're there to help you; they really are.

Chapter Eleven

Homeless by Choice?

Some people become homeless because they're too rebellious to obey normal societal rules.

I remember years ago when I was running my first shelter in Santa Fe. I had managed to obtain some temporary employment for a few weeks for one of the residents. The company who called in for a worker wanted someone for about three weeks for about sixty hours a week. They were willing to pay overtime.

Thinking it looked like a good deal, I gave the information to someone I thought would be grateful for the job and would handle himself well.

About 11:30 A.M., the shelter door opened and in walked "Joe." Very surprised, I asked him what he was doing home so early. (Wanting to believe the best, I even asked him if he was home for lunch!)

"Oh no," he replied. "That place you sent me to works you too hard. They had me lifting packing crates and a whole bunch of other stuff. I wasn't going to do that for anybody, so I just left."

"Joe" turned out to be an unmotivated individual who quickly wore out his welcome. The biggest problem with Joe was his unwillingness to admit that he had a problem!

And then there was "the prophet." His response when I asked him why he was still at the shelter at midday was that he was a prophet of God. "You should be glad I'm here!" Needless to say, he didn't last very long either! Our prerequisite for helping someone is that they want help.

You'll quickly find a lot of heartrending cases in your career as a shelter director. Treat people as individuals, be compassionate, and be aware that everyone you're dealing with is hurting. They don't need you to feel sorry for them, but neither do they need you to lord your authority over them. Your guests need to feel you're concerned and you care. Don't judge everyone alike based on one bad experience. People are different. Treat them as such!

Clients' Length of Stay

So how long should guests stay? While I'd encourage you to seek advice from other established missions, don't feel that's your only option. Some of the more established missions could be tradition-bound (in the wrong sort of way!).

I remember at a convention seminar a couple of years ago a discussion about whether shelter guests should be fed before Bible studies, or whether they should have to attend the Bible study and then be able to eat.

A couple of folks said that they believed that people responded to the gospel much better after a hamburger than they would on an empty stomach. That's also my opinion.

Put yourself in the place of those whom you're trying to help. You come to a shelter, and you're cold, tired, lonely, hungry, and afraid. Maybe you hadn't even thought of God at all. It's not that you don't believe in Him. He just doesn't seem to occupy a relevant place in your life. But one thing that you do know is that you're hungry. It's five o'clock in the evening, and after asking when the meal is, you're told that you and your family will be served after the evening service, which starts in an hour.

The hour prior to church you are all getting hungrier and hungrier. During the service, you end up paying no attention to the service and the message of God's love for you in Jesus Christ. That's because all you can think about is growling stomach pains that are getting worse and worse. In other words, the message gets lost on you.

At that convention, when some of those attending were asked why they made people sit through a gospel service before feeding them, their answer was "Because that's how we've always done it!"—not a good answer. There's nothing wrong with tradition, as long as the tradition is helpful and beneficial. But tradition for the sake of tradition is horrible!

So how long should you let people stay? Many shelters nationwide have a maximum number of days or weeks. And it is easier to do that. But if you're in this for the easiness of it, then you're in the wrong profession. Hopefully, you're doing what you're doing and reading this book because you love the Lord Jesus Christ and have a real genuine concern for people.

If you choose a three-week time limit, think about this. Let's take a family of four as our example—husband, wife, and the two children.

By a stroke of luck, the husband obtains employment the second day he's staying at your shelter. And that's really being somewhat unrealistic. It usually takes a little longer, and in many cases a lot longer, to get a job.

"Joe" gets hired by a local hotel to wash dishes. Now Joe comes on staff in the middle of the hotel's pay period, and on top of that, the hotel pays its employees every two weeks. So Joe has to go three weeks before his first paycheck.

Applying the three-week time limit, Joe will have to leave the shelter the day before he gets his first check. Even if you stretch his stay another day, there's no way that a family can get back on its feet again with the money that one wage earner will earn from a week's salary washing dishes.

So what's Joe to do? He's shown initiative in "getting out there" and getting a job. He's done everything that's possible, but "the system" has let him down. In all probability, unless there's another family shelter in town, Joe will get completely discouraged and possibly pack up his bags and family and leave town.

What will happen then? Maybe Joe and his family move onto another town where there's a really good chance of the whole cycle repeating itself. If that happens, try and imagine what this is doing to Joe's emotions and psyche. It's definitely not doing anything positive for his relationship with his wife and family, as economic tensions and pressures are already straining all the family relationships to the hilt. As this continues, Joe is beginning to get more and more depressed, until ultimately he doesn't even care if he gets a job or not. In the worse case scenario, he could lapse into some sort of clinical depression where all he wants to do is sit and stare into space. The system that should have helped Joe and his family has failed them.

A few years back, ABC-TV aired a "docudrama" about the plight of two homeless people. As I remember, it featured a woman and her child who lived in a tenement building in New York. Mom was employed as a maid at a local hotel. While the family was making ends meet, it was a tight struggle.

Things were going relatively well until the landlord announced he'd be bulldozing the apartment complex into a parking lot. That meant mom would be without a place to stay. While she looked and looked, it was all in vain. On her minimum wage job, she couldn't afford any of New York's outrageously high apartment rents and security deposits on her minimum wage job.

This lady ended up homeless. The only choice left to her was to go to a shelter. At the shelter, she faced a Victorian-looking lady staring at her over pince-nez glasses in an ogre-like fashion. The lady was quickly told that all residents had to be in by the shelter's curfew time.

She desperately tried to explain that she had a job which required her to work past the shelter curfew. The shelter operator was still unrelenting, and consequently the lady had to make a choice between shelter and a job. And why? Because that was the way the shelter had always done it. While you have to have rules, as I've said above, always remember that you're dealing with people, that people have hearts and needs, and that they're all different.

Never keep on doing something because that's the way it's always been done. On the other hand, never change a rule or policy just for the sake of change.

Rules for People or People for Rules?

You have to have rules, but have rules that are relevant. Obviously as much as you want to provide a family-type atmosphere and environment, you are still running an institution.

Joy Junction's rule-of-thumb for the length of stay is based upon the size and motivation of the family. Again, be discerning and be flexible. There's the family of dad, mom, and three kids. You notice that despite your best efforts, dad just sits around and doesn't appear to be in the least bit motivated. The only motivation he shows is a total willingness to let the shelter provide all the necessities for his wife and children. Staff are beginning to get frustrated, so you decide it's time for you to get more involved.

You begin to build a relationship with the man, and very soon a whole mass of problems begins to unfold. You learn that the reason for the lack of willingness to go out and look for work is simple but profound: The man just "freezes" when he goes in to apply for work. In the unlikely event of him getting past that first hurdle, he has no confidence about his ability to keep a job anyway.

Without telling the staff the details of a confidential counseling relationship, you tell them that this man isn't lazy but has some things going on in his life. You encourage them to go the extra mile. Love him, be very patient, and tell him that with his effort and God's help, that he will get and keep a job, and move his family out of the homeless shelter system.

You all start by giving him little jobs around the shelter which you know he can do, and you appropriately verbally reward him. Pretty soon, the man's whole demeanor and attitude begin to change, and his sense of self-worth and self-confidence begins to improve.

Then the big day finally comes, and he goes out and gets a job that he eventually keeps. Yes, you could have told him to go out and work months ago, and maybe told him that he should pull himself up and out of his financial hole by his bootstraps. But at that time he could have been emotionally incapable of fulfilling your request. The Lord, you, and your staff gave him the ability to get back on his feet and support his family again.

Even though he only has three kids, in this case, this family might need more time at the shelter than a family with a father and six kids. Perhaps the father of six kids has been laid of from a job because of purely economic reasons, and within a few short weeks, he'll be back on his feet again.

The only way you will ever discover all of this essential information is by taking time with your guests. You and your staff should cultivate relationships with them. It's only then that they'll be able to trust you enough to tell you some of the things that may have been bothering them for years.

To Preach or Not To Preach?

Bible studies (or not?)–shelters for the homeless have been traditionally started and run by evangelical Christians. The chapter on the history of shelters in America will give you more information on that very important subject.

Should you as an evangelical Christian have mandatory Bible studies, and if so, how many should you have? If you don't, will you be missing out on a golden opportunity to minister the gospel to those most in need, or do you run the risk of making homeless people gospel-hardened (especially if they've been "mission-hopping,"–going from mission to mission)?

When I started Joy Junction back in 1986, I immediately started Bible studies for six nights a week, with Saturday being a night off. We continued like that for about three or four years. Then the Lord began to "nudge" at me about changing our Bible study schedule, meaning I began to feel it was time for a change.

I was thinking along the lines of cutting down the number of Bible studies we had, making them all voluntary, or going to some other mix. One night, Rez Band was in town. They're a very successful Christian heavy metal band based out of Jesus People USA in Chicago. REZ is part of a Christian community which does a whole bunch of things, including having a shelter for homeless people, an active jail ministry, and a shelter for the aged as well.

Glenn Kaiser is the lead singer of Rez Band, and prior to that night's concert, I was talking with his wife Wendy. She was interested in our work, as those who attended the concert that night had been asked to bring a can of food to give to Joy Junction. The question of mandatory church came up, and I asked Wendy what she thought. Wendy's a very up-front lady who doesn't mince her words.

She is very opposed to forcing church upon people and said she didn't think it was something that Jesus would have done. So I listened carefully, prayed, talked to some people, and arrived at a place which I felt was right for Joy Junction.

We made the Monday, Wednesday, Thursday, and Friday services voluntary and kept the Sunday services and the Tuesday service as a must-attend. Eventually, we arrived at a variation for the Tuesday evening service. All the residents have to attend the initial few moments of the Tuesday service, basically for a roll call. After that, if they don't wish to stay, they're free to leave. About once a month, we have a special mandatory service on a Saturday. We encourage those coming to teach, preach, or sing at that service to bring cookies, goodies, or punch, and so on. At the same time we made most of the services voluntary, we told our staff that they now had a greater privilege and responsibility.

"We're not going to shove the gospel down their throats anymore," I told our staff. "So now you're going to have to work and live your life before our guests in such a way that you're going to make them curious about Jesus."

We also have a full-time Christian counselor who presents a Christian world view in his counseling sessions.

I am definitely not criticizing those shelters or agencies which choose to have Bible studies or services every day. That's their prerogative. But please be open, flexible, and obedient to the leading and guiding of the Holy Spirit. Again, this is one of those cases where as the founder and the director of a shelter, you have the ability to blaze new trails and not have nightly services just because everyone else has done it.

Staffing

Good staff will make you or break you. Before you think, "Staff?! He's out of his mind! I can't even hustle up or pray in enough money to make a livable salary for me each week. How does he think I'm going to pay STAFF?!" listen up.

Money's tight for every new ministry (or business) that starts out. You need to be able and willing to do everything in the beginning, but you won't be able to grow very much (if at all) without taking on staff. And people will judge the success of your ministry to a large extent by the manner and nature of your staff.

Where do you find these staff? As a founder and director of a shelter for the homeless, I'm assuming that you're doing what you're doing because God has called you. So the first thing to do is pray and ask God to send you the right staff: staff who will be able to catch a vision for what God has called you to do; staff who will realize that it's not their ministry, but yours; staff who feel divinely called to help empower you to effectively carry out the ministry which God has called you to do.

Having prayed and believed that God has heard and will answer your prayer, there's nothing wrong with moving full steam ahead believing that you are moving according to God's plan and direction. Here are some practical pointers to help you. Advertise with the *Happenings* publication of the International Union of Gospel Missions. Consider signing up with the Christian employment services offered by Interchristo and Bridge, Inc. Be entirely honest with potential staff. Don't "evangelically embellish," and don't offer a high salary to entice people that you have no hope of paying. If your staff are going to have to believe God for their own support (though I wouldn't recommend that), then make sure they know that well in advance of coming to you.

In other words, tell people everything—the worst-case scenarios—before you hire them. It'll save you a whole lot of grief afterwards. If a potential staffer is married, meet both halves of the couple and be sure both are aware of these critical issues.

I don't recommend that you have your staff raise their own support, and one reason is that it tends to diminish their accountability to you. They begin to think that they're working for themselves instead of you because they're raising their own salary. Remember that people aren't automatically good workers (unfortunately) just because they call themselves Christians. They should be, but my experience in many cases has been that the exact opposite applies.

On salaries: You'll usually get whatever you pay for. It's OK if you can only pay minimum wage, but be aware that professional personnel usually come with professional prices. A shelter can get by with a lot of unskilled personnel, but you still need some skilled professionals for key positions.

Don't skimp on the quality of whomever you have to answer your phone–and please, please, please don't try and go cheap on your business manager. As I've shared, I learned at great cost and by very painful experience that a good business manager is the key to continuing success. (Obviously all of my suggestions are only hypothetical until you can produce the income to allow them to become a reality!)

Using Former Residents for Staff

Should you use former homeless residents to staff the shelter? From what I've gathered, it seems to be a pretty common practice. But let me suggest something a little more practical.

Joy Junction formed a life-skills program for some of our residents. We named it POPI–Program Participants Initiative. Several aspects comprise the program. It offers training in maintenance, cooking, driving, and supervision, etc. Many of the residents who come to us have some pretty basic work skills, but they lack the social skills to allow effective functioning of the work skills. That naturally renders people rather ineffective in the work force.

So we take people who have, for example, some basic cooking skills but maybe have a problem relating to their boss' position of authority. In a regular work setting, maybe their boss tells them to perform a specific duty, which is well within their ability to perform. Instead of cheerfully obeying, they unleash a string of profanity and tell their boss they have no intention of doing anything he says. Well, naturally enough, they get fired. The POPI training teaches them to obey their boss. The individual would be informed that if they want to function in society, they can't act like that and expect to make it. POPI also teaches basic skills like clocking in and clocking out, coming to work on time, communicating and not reacting, and so on.

Some of the residents enrolled in POPI also get assigned to what we call "floor staff." Basically, what that means is that they help staff check in residents, relate to other homeless people in crisis situations, and learn some basic "people-coping skills." They also assist in helping take care of basic needs, like getting shampoo, deodorant, diapers, and overseeing order. If any problems occur, the individual's instructions are to immediately find a staff member and not to try to solve it by himself. We also hope that POPI participants will use some preventative skills and attempt to ensure that problems don't happen by keeping a watchful eye at all times.

So do we use residents as staff? Not really–just in the sense I've described above as resident trainees. Our training program helps us help the homeless more effectively. If you have a training program, make sure there is plenty of Bible study and classroom training, i.e., the theory as well as the practical. Make sure that you don't take advantage of those whom you're trying to help. You're running a training program, not a cheap labor program.

Using homeless people in any supervisory capacity over other homeless people is something that has to be watched very carefully. You wouldn't necessarily think so, but some formerly homeless people tend to be very cruel in their dealings with currently homeless people. It's as if the power goes to their head.

Remember, if you do use homeless people for staff, just because you've upgraded a person to staff status, thus making them technically not homeless, it doesn't mean that the "homeless" has been taken out of them. Homelessness is a state of mind as well as a state of being.

When Do You Ask Rule Breakers to Leave?

When do you ask someone to leave? Let's look at a situation where someone violates the no-drinking policy. Do you automatically ask them to leave? Or not?

Again, I would suggest that you treat everyone individually and not uniformly. Let me explain. I'm sure that your shelter will have a no-drinking policy. In some cases, it's alcohol consumption that has resulted in people becoming homeless. But say you have an alcoholic staying at the shelter. A twenty-year alcoholic, while not necessarily drinking right now, is still someone with a twenty-year history of drinking behind him. He might be able to stay clean for a few months and might be someone who impresses you so much that you put him in a position of responsibility. Then he blows it, doesn't check into the shelter for a few days, and the next thing you hear about him is a report from the police saying he's in the drunk tank.

If he's a single man, it's seemingly an easy decision to throw him out since he's violated your no-alcohol policy. Even then (and I know a lot of you will probably disagree with me on this point), I don't necessarily think you should throw someone out for one violation. At this point, don't throw up your hands and scream in a sanctimonious fashion, "How can he say that? Does he want us to encourage drinking?"

I most definitely don't. Rather I hope you will act like Christ and show His love and compassion. I don't want you to make decisions and act in such a way that you'll make people gospel-hardened by hypocritical and bigoted acts. If you have a twenty-year veteran alcoholic, it took him twenty years to get that way. While he might change instantaneously, in all probability he's not going to. It will take awhile. Jesus was patient with you in your maybe-not-quite-so-open sins. Can you be as patient with an overt alcoholic?

Now let's go back to our husband, wife, and children. Mom tries really hard, but all dad wants to do is sit around, one of the sort of guys who thinks the world owes him a living and that he's God's blessing to mankind. The kids are going to school, mom is trying really hard, but dad is the thorn in everyone's side. He won't work, and maybe he even beats mom up. You throw him out, but mom lets him back in the window at night. What do you do? Do you throw everyone out and thus put a couple of innocent kids on the street? Are you encouraging dad in his abuse and other bad habits if you let the situation ride? It's a hard situation, isn't it, without any easy answers?

Even as Christians, we want to have easy, pat answers. You know, black and whites and no grays. And while there are absolutes for human morals and behavior, in a situation like this, especially where there are so many people involved, the waters become really muddy.

Treat people like individuals and make your decision prayerfully and fairly based upon what you believe is an appropriate and just response to their situation. Obviously you must have a working policy and a no-alcohol policy, and they should be enforced. The point I'm trying to make here is that they must be open-enough policies to allow people to be treated as individuals.

In summary: Be flexible, rely on your gut feelings, common sense, and the leading of the Holy Spirit. Remember that the homeless situation in America is in a state of flux because the homeless "situation" is made up of people. As the "situation" changes, change with it!

Chapter Twelve

Many Poor People— But Only One of You

The Bible says the poor we shall always have with us. That translates to overwhelming need (on a consistent basis). And you're always going to have young, unwed ladies getting pregnant, alcoholics, and youngsters who need a Christian education, as well as people who need to be pastored. Don't be overwhelmed by the need but let it motivate you to do greater things and encourage you to go on to greater heights.

There's always going to be an overwhelming need, but there's only one of you. Additionally, you are limited by the resources with which God entrusts you. As great as the need seems, it's still more important to be obedient to God. God is more impressed by your obedience (or otherwise) to Him than by the scale of what you do.

When you incorporated as a non-profit corporation, you had to formulate what's known as a "mission statement." That says in a sentence or two what you're all about. It's the reason for your existence. Hold yourself to that statement. It will help you stay right on track. I'm assuming you are an intelligent, disciplined, skilled, and motivated person. There are probably a number of career choices that you could have followed, had you not chosen to be obedient to the Lord's calling upon your life and embark on full-time ministry.

But ministry, or "people work," is somewhat intangible. It's not like you start a particular task and finish a few hours or a few days later. *You don't.* Dealing with people is like being a spoke in a giant wheel. In this case you're making an investment in the life of a person, the full fruits of which might not be seen for many years to come. And in most cases you'll never see the tangible results of what you accomplish.

That takes me back to a theme of this book. Before you embark on this work, you MUST make sure that you have a definite calling to do so. The "calling," which could manifest in a variety of ways, is what will keep you going through the hard times.

When you begin to feel that you need thanks, remember why you're in ministry. You're (hopefully) being obedient to God, so it has to be God who gives you the thanks. You're in this business for the wrong reason if you're looking for thanks from clients. (That may happen occasionally, but treat it as icing on the cake.)

As we've discussed above, the need is always going to be there. It's always been there, and it will continue to be there until Jesus comes. Sometimes the trauma and drama of the need will get to you. You'll see some of the same people coming back again in the same desperate straits year after year. Sometimes things will seem especially frustrating, as you know that there's no work to be found by hanging around the shelter and just "goofing off."

You also wonder at some people's inappropriate choices, like the seeming inability or unwillingness of alcoholics to rely on the Lord and stay away from bars. You get depressed when someone you really thought was on the way back up blows it and goes out and gets drunk.

Leaving It with the Lord

You know that if people would just give their lives to Jesus that He would help them work through all the crises they're having. You know that the Lord wants to step in and fill the emotional void in their lives and help them kick the bad habits and get out of the slump.

But how do you communicate that knowledge so it reaches their heart? All you can do is share what you believe with those to whom you minister, and then leave the ultimate results to the Lord. It's your responsibility to share the answers to problems encountered by your guests. But you can't hold yourself responsible, and I don't believe God holds you responsible, for what your needy guests do with the information you give them.

If you don't leave the ultimate results in the Lord's hands, you run the risk of losing your emotional sanity. Remember the Scripture: "Cast your burdens upon the Lord and leave them there"? Do it. Love your guests with the love of the Lord, pray for them, do everything you possibly can for them, but realize your limitations. God is sovereign, but you aren't. There comes a time when you have to step back and leave these people in the Lord's hands.

I'm sure that you're in ministry because you love God and people, and you have a genuine calling and desire to reach out to the needy with the love of Jesus Christ. Now if you pastor a church, the situation isn't quite the same, but it is similar. You have a bunch of people who need pastoring–or shepherding. While they probably have a roof over their heads, and most of them have a job, they still have lots of problems–they're just not quite so obvious. And as a pastor, how do you feel when you invest a lot of time in someone, and they turn their back on you and leave the church. Or perhaps you've spent hundreds of hours on, say, marriage counseling a couple, and they just go out and get a divorce. It hurts, doesn't it?

If you're anything like me, I'm also sure that you've put in a lot of unnoticed, unrewarded, and unpaid hours at the ministry. I'd also hazard a guess that if your entrepreneurial skills were being used in a secular setting, you could be making a lot more money than you are presently running a church or a para-church ministry. But you do what you do because of your love for Jesus and people, right?

So what's your reaction going to be when one day you hear that the homeless (or church members or clients or whomever you minister to) whom you're spending your life serving are telling horrible untruths about you to everyone in town?

During the almost seven years Joy Junction's been in existence, we've been accused of an amazing number of things, including serving drug-contaminated food to residents so we can make them our "slaves."

The shelter sits on a large acreage, and a few years ago I was told one of the rumors circulating around the homeless community. They were saying we serve poisoned food to residents, and we bury those who die in the backfields. (They must be the ones who refuse to be our slaves.)

The kitchen crew get a lot of the criticism; I guess because what they do is so visible and open. The criticism continues despite the staff trying to make nourishing, appetizing meals with the food the shelter is given.

One day a local hotel started giving us food. The second day's food was sweet and sour pork. A comment overheard from one resident: "I wouldn't feed that to my dog." Think how disheartening it can be when, as the founder and director of a shelter, you've put your life into serving the homeless—or your cook's spent hours cooking the best meal possible, and nasty comments are made about it. At times like that, even if you and all your staff know that you have a definite calling from the Lord to be in shelter-care ministry, it could still be tempting to lose it. But you've got to respond and not react.

The same thing applies to whomever you're serving. Try and realize that because you're where you are, the dysfunctional people you serve are taking their anger about their life's circumstances out on you. They're caught in the middle of a string of unfortunate circumstances which they presently can't do anything about. But there are many homeless people who need to have a scapegoat, and who better to blame all their problems on than you as the caregiver? And who are *we* nastiest to in life? Usually those who care most for us.

If you realize the dynamics of the situation and act accordingly, you'll have more of a chance of not burning out. If you burnout, you can't help anyone. I know there's that old saying "I'd rather burn out than rust out for Jesus," but if you burn or rust, you're still going to be out of commission for the Lord.

Realize that you can't do everything for everyone. There must be a list of priorities. Here they are as I see them: God is first, followed by your wife and children, and your ministry comes next–or last.

Church Attendance (Not for "Them," But for You)

You need a church that's going to meet the needs of your whole family. I've met wonderfully committed shelter directors who absolutely refuse to make a commitment to a church. Their rationale is that they need to meet as many people as possible to PR the shelter. They bounce from one local church to the next, never making a commitment to any.

Flitting from church to church might help the shelter by giving you a little more exposure. However, I firmly believe you need to make a commitment to a local church, become involved, and stick with it. Try and limit yourself to going out very occasionally on Sunday mornings to speak about the shelter. God's going to bless you, your family, and the ministry accordingly.

Church commitment will be a blessing to your wife and children because they'll see you're putting their spiritual needs first. They need to see that their needs don't take a back seat to everyone else's. I know it's very easy for that to happen when coping with the demands of a busy ministry. Make your church commitment prayerfully and carefully. You need to honor your commitment once you've made it. Just because the pastor says something that offends you is no excuse for leaving. (And he might never ask you to share the needs of your ministry either!)

Sharing Time

Consider joining a church home fellowship and sharing some of your concerns and burdens with the members. Now notice that I say "some." As a para-church executive, there will be certain trials and struggles you face to which no one except someone familiar with the trials and struggles of ministry will be able to relate. Don't make the mistake of telling too much to the wrong people and risk the chance of having it thrown back at you. But if you do say too much to too many, or you've told the wrong person and gotten burned, don't clam up and refuse to speak to anyone. That won't help anyone either, you included.

While you definitely need a pastor, don't be surprised if he doesn't understand all the strains and stresses associated with running para-church ministry–anymore than you understand what it's like to pastor a church! If any pastors or potential pastors are reading this, I would encourage you to try and relate to the emotional and spiritual strains faced by para-church management. And to you shelter or drug rehab types, it's not all that easy pastoring a church either. You need to understand the strains and stresses faced by your pastor.

I've found that most pastors don't understand the cyclical giving pattern experienced by para-church ministries. Pastors have more of an established and consistent income because of the tithe variable. So in addition to your pastor, find another person (maybe another para-church ministry executive) to talk to. Once you begin to share trials and struggles, you'll find that much of what you go through, with a few variations, is common to many other ministries. The outward trappings are different, but the root causes and the solutions are very similar. If you don't share problems, you'll begin to think that you're the only person going through these things.

Join the International Union of Gospel Missions if you're a shelter operator, or find another "trade group." The IUGM is an affiliated, loose-knit group of rescue ministries that get together regionally and nationally for fellowship, conventions, seminars, and more. The IUGM could be a tremendous benefit to you. They can be very useful for quick, readily accessible advice. Sometimes things come up for which you just have to have an immediate answer. To whom do you turn? On numerous occasions, I've turned to the IUGM. The advice given and the money and time saved has made the yearly membership fee well worth it.

Many cities have a ministerial alliance. I'd suggest you join that, especially if it's evangelical. A group like that can be a great tool for networking and getting the word out about the mission, crisis pregnancy center, meal site, etc. And then other cities have groups like one we have here in Albuquerque, called the Albuquerque Care Alliance. That's a group of local emergency service providers that get together on a regular basis for networking and encouragement.

If there are other evangelicals in your city, I'd recommend you start an informal alliance where every so often you get together for prayer and fellowship and maybe a meal. God's continued blessing and encouragement from like-minded brothers and sisters will help keep you going in times of stress.

The Critics

Those times of stress will come when those (and you get them in secular business as well as Christian ministry) who think they could run your ministry so much better than you can begin to criticize you.

My former shelter in Santa Fe was basically a one-man operation. I worked long hours, took four days off in as many years, and had one street person at a time helping me. While the ministry was very rewarding, it was also physically and emotionally demanding.

One day, I was visiting with a donor who suddenly told me, "Well, you know why the [and he named some individuals] don't come anymore, don't you?"

I had to confess that I didn't know. Actually, I wasn't sure I really wanted to know, but she told me anyway.

"Well, the last time they were here, they said the bathrooms were absolutely filthy, and they just weren't going to come down to a place that looked like that. They said it wouldn't be that way if they were in charge."

The criticism hurt because here I was working so many hours, and these critical people couldn't even tell me their problem face to face. All they could do was criticize the shelter to others and quit coming to help.

I've experienced numerous cases over the years of people who thought they could do a better job than me. If you haven't experienced the same phenomenon, don't worry. Sooner or later (probably sooner) you will. My advice to you is, tell these people: "I'm doing the best I can. If you can do better, there's room for two of us." You won't hear much more from them. Most workers are too busy to criticize, and most critics are too busy to work.

But don't get mad with these folk because even criticism delivered in the wrong spirit has some truth to it. There was truth to the bathrooms being dirty. But it would have been a whole lot nicer if those critics had been a little more perceptive and had offered their services to clean the bathrooms for us.

They were shortsighted people who just couldn't see beyond the immediate—dirty bathrooms. They weren't willing to ask why there were dirty bathrooms, they just wanted an excuse to criticize. There will always be people like that, but once you've suffered at their hands, it will hopefully give you a double motivation not to be like them.

Usually your most strident critics will be those who are jealous of you but aren't sufficiently motivated to do anything else except slam those who are doing well. Use those—and all—critics as a learning and growing experience.

Chapter Thirteen

Keeping the Vision

So now you have a shelter, or whatever the particular ministry that God laid on your heart to begin. You've dreamed, prayed, imagined, believed, and performed every sort of spiritual calisthenic possible to make this day a reality. And it's finally here!

I've always found that there's more thrill in anticipating an event than when you actually get to its arrival. In fact, sometimes the event can almost be a downer. So unless you've started already, you need to develop a vision for the future beyond the stand opening and the expansion of your ministry. You must have something to dream and hope for.

As I've already tried to stress in some detail, you must also have a personal vision. That's not just what God wants for the future of the ministry, but what He wants for you as well in relation to that ministry (and any other project in which He might have you participate).

You'll discover that when the thrill of being the director of a ministry wears off, it can be compared in some ways to marriage. When you get married, initially you believe that your spouse doesn't have a fault in the world. You're all starry-eyed about each other. All you want to do is to spend time in each other's company. But then you find out that you both have faults and maybe some chronic bad habits. You know, husbands, those little things that really bother her, like not putting the toilet seat down and leaving clothes all over the floor. The only way any marriage survives is as a result of commitment.

You don't leave your wife because you wake up one day and feel that you don't love her. You've made a commitment to love her. And in the same way that you stick with marriage, you stick with ministry. You do it because of the calling that you've had from God and because you want to obey that calling. Now just like marriage, sometimes there'll be good days, and again just like marriage, sometimes there will be bad days. Commitment and obedience are the two key words.

I regard any thanks that I get from anyone as icing on the cake. I started Joy Junction and continue running Joy Junction because I firmly believe that I am obeying a divine calling of God on my life to minister to the homeless.

Something that will help you hang in there is attending local meetings. There are two types that could be available in your community. Sometimes evangelically oriented shelter providers meet together once a month or so. Then there are the others of a more liberal persuasion. I've been to meetings with some liberally oriented shelter providers in attendance where the subject of the homeless scarcely comes up. I would strongly encourage you to join the former. Draw on them for encouragement. If there's no such meeting, then consider starting one. You'll be surprised how much encouragement you'll get even from an occasional gathering.

Somehow you need to orchestrate a meeting with people who understand the problems peculiar to your ministry. Many para-church executives don't have any idea of the pressures that go along with pastoring a church—especially a small one—and vice versa. I don't mean that you spend all of your time attending meetings; that would be counterproductive. Any encouragement that you glean at meetings would immediately dissipate upon return to the office and the sight of the work that had accumulated in your absence.

In particular, I don't usually attend task force meetings. I've been asked to be on several and have usually ended up dropping out. They can consume a tremendous amount of time, and my personal opinion is that in many cases the recommendations that they arrive at do little good. However, you may feel differently.

Getting and Staying Noticed

As well as "hanging in there" and making sure you stay personally encouraged, you must also work out how you can keep a high profile in the community. This is very important if you decide not to receive any government funding. And I'd recommend eschewing federal, state, county, or city funding. It could create conflict with any religious program you want to set up in the shelter because of the dubious separation of church and state position.

So if you go the no-public-funding route, you'll be relying on the private sector, and one of your main jobs will be to remind the private sector continually, in new and creative ways, that you're there. The squeaky wheel gets attention, but a wheel that always squeaks in the same way becomes an annoyance. So you have to work out ways that you can stay in the limelight. You have to give the press a reason for wanting to cover you, as well as your donors a reason for wanting to give to you.

However, there are also dangers in being "high-profile." To some extent, your ministry and you as a person almost become public property. Unless you are very careful, you risk being high-profile in a manner in which you hadn't bargained.

Coping with Bad Press—Accepting Responsibility

This happened to us at Joy Junction. I've shared some of this at length in the first chapter, so what I'm going to share with you here is the entire set of local publicity in all its ugly detail and how I coped with it.

There was one thing I did which I didn't realize the importance of until after the event—I accepted responsibility for the whole mess and moved swiftly and resolutely to solve the crisis situation. Just as the shelter got out of the situation, by using that same technique, so can you.

Before we get into the articles, I've already mentioned approaches that will help you cope with bad press: accepting responsibility, being obedient to your commitment, having a strong, ongoing relationship with the Lord, and attending meetings and becoming known to your peers so they'll be able to help you and stand with you through a time of crisis.

Here is the first article in mid 1990, written by *Albuquerque Journal* staff reporter Leah Lorber. It was headlined "'Seats of Pants' Finances Land Joy Junction in Hole."

> Joy Junction, Albuquerque's largest shelter for homeless families, is seeking donations to pay nearly $20,000 in unpaid bills and shore up its shaky finances.
>
> At the same time the shelter is attempting to shore up what its director calls "seat of the pants" financial practices, which have been handled on a month to month basis, with no annual budget.
>
> Joy Junction's books for 1989 and 1990 reveal poor record keeping, bounced checks, unpaid bills and unpaid taxes. They also show the shelter donated more than $20,000 last year to other organizations, most of which are out of state.
>
> The director, the Rev. Jeremy Reynalds, said he has been meeting with Albuquerque business people to improve the shelter's financial management. He said he has tightened check-writing procedures and hired an accounting firm to audit the books. He also plans to hire a part-time business manager.
>
> Reynalds blamed the problems on his trying to do too many jobs, his limited business experience, and the shelter's rapid expansion.
>
> "I don't put the blame for our failings . . . on anyone else," he said.
>
> Reynalds said that unless he can raise $20,000 by July 31, the shelter will close.
>
> The donations for the first four months of this year totalled $87,683, compared to about $70,000 over the same period last year.
>
> While the number of residents declined slightly, expenses rose sharply because of a larger payroll. The number of employees increased from nine to 20 be-

> tween March 1989 and March 1990 because of expanded services, according to shelter officials.
>
> As of Friday, the shelter had $2,201 in the bank and owed $19,290.
>
> Larry Lanphere, the shelter's volunteer tax accountant, said he's warned Reynalds about sloppy record-keeping.
>
> "Jeremy has a beautiful heart, but he's not a financial manager," said Lanphere, who does not handle the shelter's bookkeeping.
>
> Lanphere said that despite the problem, he supports the shelter's mission, a feeling echoed by others throughout the city.
>
> "Joy Junction is the major provider for emergency shelter services to homeless families," said Michael Passi, who oversees the city's support to social service agencies. "It would be very regrettable if the service were lost even temporarily in Albuquerque."
>
> Hospitals, law enforcement agencies and other shelters refer families to Joy Junction, which housed 3,434 people last year.
>
> "They're a valuable resource to the police department," said Capt. Sal Baragiola of Albuquerque Police Department's valley substation. "If any of these shelters were to close, it would be detrimental to the police department's ability to handle the homeless problem."

The article went on to detail some specific problems. Let's take it up again here:

> The shelter serves between 80 and 100 homeless adults and children a night, Reynalds said.
>
> The shelter runs on money from private donations and does not accept money from the state, city or federal government. It is not a United Way agency, although some people donate to the shelter through the United Way program.
>
> "What he's doing now is seeing himself start falling further behind," Lanphere said. "You can only put the check in the mail so many times . . . when they don't

believe you and you can't even say it sincerely anymore."

Reynalds said Joy Junction first operated with a small staff that worked a lot of overtime. But demands for more service–and employee burnout–forced him to hire more employees and pay for more work hours.

The amount of Joy Junction's quarterly payroll rose from about $6,000 in March 1989 to about $21,000 a year later, Lanphere said. Those figures do not include Reynalds' salary.

Reynalds said he makes $300 a week, and is provided housing on the Joy Junction property. His utility bills, between $100 and $125 a month, are also paid for by Joy Junction, and he has personal use of one of the shelter's nine vehicles. He said he moonlights at two local radio stations to raise enough money to support his six-member family.

The shelter includes a main hall with fold-out couches, a makeshift worship area, and adjacent private rooms. A separate dormitory provides rooms for women. In addition to the $20,000 Reynalds is seeking immediately, he is also trying to find 1,200 people who would commit to donating $20 a month.

"I would hope that Joy Junction can do some strategic planning, both in terms of developing a financial management system and in terms of services," Passi said. "Presuming they can do that, and demonstrate to the public they have done that, I see no reason for (donors) not continuing to support Joy Junction."

Reynalds also hopes to improve Joy Junction's services to help homeless people make new lives. He plans to phase in such programs as regular, financial, health and substance abuse counseling. (Used by permission.)

Whew! I've already described how I felt about this article in the first chapter, but now you can read for yourself the article almost in its entirety. To say I was devastated would be an understatement. At the time this article was printed, I had run shelters for eight years with nothing but positive press. This article was at the top of that Saturday's *Journal* along with what I felt was a very unflattering picture of me.

I dreaded going to the office that morning, but I went anyway. Naturally, the phone rang (off the hook!). Most people weren't as upset about the unpaid bills, late payments on taxes, or bounced checks as they were about the "tithing." That really upset people. Something I felt very strongly about doing in honor to God had been taken totally the wrong way.

A close friend explained it like this. "Jeremy, they felt they were giving to help the homeless in Albuquerque, specifically those staying at Joy Junction. They feel cheated because the money wasn't going for that purpose." Having someone else explain that made sense, and I began to see how my actions looked to others.

One of the phone calls that Saturday morning was from someone who volunteered her services as a business manager, which we gratefully accepted.

I also made an immediate decision to have a community meeting and expand our board, but before I had the opportunity to do much, there was more press in the *The Albuquerque Journal*. This time it was a caustic editorial.

> Joy Junction, Albuquerque's largest shelter for homeless families, is in dire need of a cash infusion to shore up its shaky finances. As a *Journal* report of the handling of its finances makes clear, it is also in need of an infusion of business management.
>
> The Rev. Jeremy Reynalds, Joy Junction director, is working on both problems. He is meeting with Albuquerque business people to improve the shelter's financial structure and has hired an accounting firm to audit the books. At the same time, Reynalds warns, if Joy Junction doesn't raise $20,000 by July 31, the shelter will close. As of last Friday, the shelter had $2,201 in the bank and owed $19,290.
>
> "Joy Junction is the major provider for emergency shelter services to homeless families," said Michael Passi, who oversees the city's financial support to social service agencies. "It would be very regrettable if the service were lost even temporarily."

> But if Reynalds' motivation is beyond reproach, his business sense leaves much to be desired.
>
> Joy Junction has not had a formal budget or a financial director since it incorporated in 1987. Finances are handled month to month.
>
> During 1989, Joy Junction donated about $26,000 to other organizations, even as it was falling behind on its own obligations. Reynalds said the donations stopped about two months ago.
>
> Check writing procedures were so loose that employees had been allowed to take blank checks to purchase items, sometimes forgetting to record the item, causing several checks to bounce.
>
> Reynalds has taken several steps to bring order to Joy Junction's financial organization. It should be a priority for him.
>
> Reynalds and Joy Junction provide an indispensable service to Albuquerque's homeless. He must also provide a financial structure sufficient to enjoy the confidence of Albuquerqueans he calls on to support Joy Junction with their contributions. (*The Albuquerque Journal*, 1990. Used by permission.)

That editorial hurt more than the article. But as a close friend told me the morning of the first article, "Jeremy, God can use this to the good. There's been no mention of malfeasance or misappropriation. This article could be the best thing that ever happened to you!"

And it turned out to be. One of the people that called the Saturday morning the article was published said, "How can we help? You've been doing too much for too many with too little for too long. Reading that article this morning made me realize that."

Hopefully, you're beginning to see how you should handle bad or questionable press. The two main points are: acknowledge your responsibility as the head of the organization and act swiftly and decisively to bring about any needed changes.

Here's some of the second article that appeared a few days later, also by *The Albuquerque Journal* staff reporter Leah Lorber.

Joy Junction, Albuquerque's largest shelter for homeless families, has selected a part-time business manager and raised about $6,500 of the $20,000 needed to pay off its overdue bills.

In addition, local business people are scheduled to meet with shelter operators next week to discuss how to improve Joy Junction's internal management, said the shelter's executive director, the Rev. Jeremy Reynalds.

"We've made some mistakes," Reynalds said. "We're jumping on the problems immediately to restore any lost confidence the community has in this. We're looking at a total reorganization of the whole (management) structure."

Reynalds said the business director, Lauri Behrends, will officially start after her hiring is formally approved next week by all three board members.

Behrends, a former administrator and bookkeeper from Service Steam, Inc., of Albuquerque said she has had eight years of experience in finance and accounting.

"I have no doubt in my leadership ability," she said. "I feel I can handle the job."

Behrends, 28, said her goals include computerizing Joy Junction's accounting system, organizing employees' time and outlining their job descriptions.

Reynalds said that writing a budget will be among her first tasks.

He added that Behrends has promised to work for free until she has studied and computerized the shelter's books since 1986, Reynalds said.

"I would only consider a salary after everything is up and running," said Behrends. "I'm really not interested in a salary. It's not important."

Reynalds said they have not settled on a final salary.

Joy Junction also intends to expand its board from three members to seven to get more community input, Reynalds said.

Reynalds is now executive director and president of the board. The other board members are Rev. Gino Geraci

> of Calvary Chapel and Mark Oberman, Reynalds' assistant director.
>
> "I need more insight and input from the financial community," Reynalds said. "I'm doing too much for too many with too few resources."
>
> The shelter may also set up a financial advisory board of local business people. (*The Albuquerque Journal*, 1990. Used by permission.)

You see that we took quick and decisive action. I obviously believed that the problems we faced were extremely serious. That was one thing. I also had to make the community understand that I realized the seriousness of the problems.

This was the next article that appeared. It was headlined "Homeless Shelter Adds Financial Advisory Board," also by *The Albuquerque Journal* reporter Leah Lorber.

> Joy Junction, Albuquerque's largest shelter for homeless families, has expanded its executive board and added a financial advisory board to help improve its internal management.
>
> In addition, the shelter has raised about $32,000 to pay overdue bills and current operating expenses since a fund-raising drive began in mid-June, said the shelter's director, Jeremy Reynalds.
>
> "We're very happy with the community response to the emergency cash need, and we'll do our very best to carry out everything that the community expects us to do in a responsible fashion," said Reynalds.
>
> But he warned that the shelter will close unless 400-500 people agree by July 31 to make monthly donations. Services would be cut back unless 1,000 people promise steady donations, but Reynalds is seeking 1,200 donors to allow the shelter to expand its bed space and services.
>
> The promise of a steady income would allow the shelter's new business manager to write a budget and put the shelter on stable financial ground, Reynalds said.
>
> Reynalds wants the 1,200 donors to pledge $20 a month for a total $288,000 a year. The shelter received $262,000

in 1989 and spent $237,000. Since the fund-raiser started, Reynalds has received 52 pledges totalling about $1,300 a month.

The shelter is in the midst of trying to straighten out its tangled finances, which have been run month-to-month without an annual budget. The shelter's financial problems included bounced checks, unpaid bills and unpaid taxes.

The shelter's financial problems stemmed from its rapid expansion, said Reynalds, combined with his limited business experience and his trying to do too many jobs. In late June he hired a former administrator and bookkeeper for Service Steam, Inc., of Albuquerque, Lauri Behrends, as business manager.

The next section of the article was very important. It listed the occupations of board members, designed to help restore confidence.

The new members of the executive board are Rick La Strapes, a Rio Rancho attorney, Michael Stitzell, the general manager of KKIM Radio, Larry Austin, Albuquerque branch manager of Shearson, Lehman Hutton, the Rev. Carl Conley, pastor of Santa Fe Community Church and President of the Life Link in Santa Fe; and Reynalds and his wife Sylvia. A seventh person has not decided whether to become a board member, Reynalds said.

Reynalds said he has stepped down as board president.

In addition, he said, two people will serve as executive board advisors. They are Mike Kull, the president of New Mexico Boys and Girls Ranch Foundation, and Gino Geraci, the associate pastor of Calvary Chapel.

Now look again at the members of the financial advisory board. We made a public commitment to seek more community input, and we did just that.

These are Gary and Linda Hays, the owners of Cliff's Amusement Park, Ralph Sanchez, a city of Albuquerque planner and analyst; Frank Casanova, the president of Sunland Management; Linda Casanova, a local architect; and Deborah and Victor Tate, insurance agents

> with Mass. Mutual Life Insurance Co. An eighth person is considering joining the board, Reynalds said. (*The Albuquerque Journal*, 1990. Used by permission.)

After the articles, many people in the community were still behind me, but even some of those thought that I had the financial acumen of a billygoat. They had to be convinced in particular, and the community in general, that I was receiving sound input and advice from the community.

If you ever set up an advisory board, either to cope with the effects of bad press or for any other reason, make sure those on the board are fully aware that they are an *advisory* board–they are not the corporation's *governing* board.

A few months later, I met with our board president concerning the financial advisory board. The board's decision was to disband the advisory board.

"Thank them for their services," board president Carl Conley said. "But then tell them that your original reason for wanting such a board was to seek additional financial advice, which at the time you were lacking. Now that you have that, you don't need them. Public trust should be in you and the board."

I also found a wonderful business manager. This man, who still works for me, is a former Assemblies of God pastor and a former financial big-wig with the state of New Mexico. Whereas I enjoy nothing more than talking to reporters and being on radio and television, this man is a precision-oriented, detail man. Frank likes doing tax returns at two o'clock in the morning. And believe me, Frank keeps us all in line.

I never before realized the importance of a business manager, but listen up. While your shelter is still small, get someone other than you to handle all the books and the finances. Set up written policies and procedures. And remember: Even if you and your wife started off the shelter, it is not your own personal business once you are registered as a non-profit with a tax-exempt determination from the Internal Revenue Service.

Realizing the need for a business manager was a direct spin-off from the "negative" press. I firmly believe that what the devil intended for evil, and maybe the possible demise of the shelter, God turned around and used for good. The whole process was also a reminder to me that perhaps I had too readily taken for granted eight years of positive press.

In addition, if you keep a high-public profile and enjoy the benefits thereof, you have to realize that you are placing yourself in a position of great public accountability, and a business manager helps you have nothing to hide.

Joy Junction in the News–Continued

Anyway, here is the next story in the "series" about how things progressed. This time it was in Albuquerque's afternoon paper, the *Albuquerque Tribune*, written by staff reporter Ed Asher.

> Joy Junction, Albuquerque's largest shelter for homeless families, has survived a budget crisis, and its director says he hopes he will be able to keep the shelter running.
>
> "As of now, I'm cautiously optimistic that we'll be able to keep it open, with the probability that we'll have to reduce some of the services we provide for our residents," shelter director Jeremy Reynalds said Sunday.
>
> In early June, Reynalds made a public plea for donations to pay overdue bills and monthly operating expenses. He predicted that he might have to close the shelter by the end of the month.
>
> Since June 6, Joy Junction has raised $64,898–enough to pay off some bills and head off the impending shutdown, he said.
>
> The shelter, which can handle about 100 people a night and currently houses 85 people, costs $22,000 to $25,000 a month to operate, he said.
>
> But even the recent contributions aren't enough to guarantee the shelter's continued existence, he said.
>
> Without donors willing to commit to making monthly donations, the shelter may have to reduce services, including cutting the amount of services it now provides to its residents.

> Reynalds is attempting to persuade 1,200 people to pledge $20 a month, to raise $288,000 a year.
>
> The guaranteed payments would allow the shelter's new business manager to write a budget and put the shelter on stable financial ground.
>
> As of late last week, 271 people had pledged a total of $6,688 a month.
>
> "We have a sizable number of people who give every month, but who don't want to make a commitment," he said.
>
> "But I expect that by Tuesday, our self-imposed deadline, we'll have a bunch of new pledges." (The *Albuquerque Tribune*, 1990. Used by permission.)

As you see, the perception being given to the community by the press was that we were making progress, and that perception was entirely accurate. We were and have been continuing to make steady progress ever since.

However, I knew and so did the *Albuquerque Journal*, that there needed to be some sort of follow-up to the problems that had been aired in the initial article. The issue wouldn't have been really resolved without that. So in November 1990, the follow-up came. It was headlined "Homeless Shelter Writes 1st Budget, Adds Spending Controls," by staff reporter Leah Lorber.

> Joy Junction has written its first annual budget and put in place internal spending controls as part of an overhaul of the homeless shelter's financial practices.
>
> The shelter's new business manager, Francisco Tercero, also is reconstructing financial records and an audit will be performed in 1991.
>
> "We have to show the community that what we are is what we say we are," said the Rev. Jeremy Reynalds, Joy Junction's executive director. "We have to show integrity in the way we handle donors money."
>
> The shelter for families has taken several steps to improve what Reynalds in June called "seat of the pants" financial practices, which were handled month-to-month

with no annual budget. The shelter's financial problems included bounced checks, unpaid bills and unpaid taxes.

Reynalds attributed the shelter's financial problems to its rapid expansion, his limited business experience and his trying to do too many jobs.

Joy Junction this summer reorganized its management structure, expanding its board members from three to six to get more community input and setting up a financial advisory board made up of Reynalds and seven local business people.

The shelter in August hired Tercero as business manager. A 17-year state employee, he worked for three-and-a-half years as chief fiscal officer under then-Attorney General Toney Anaya.

As well as working to computerize and reconstruct Joy Junction's financial records, Tercero set up internal spending controls. The new spending controls are in addition to steps such as tightening check-writing practices that Reynalds took this summer.

For example, now Tercero approves and writes checks. Reynalds is the only shelter official who can sign the checks after giving them his final approval.

The shelter's petty cash fund always must have either a set amount of cash, or cash and receipts totalling that amount.

Staff members using the shelter's vehicles must sign a log book noting such information as the mileage, the reason for the trip, and the time it was taken. Staff members wishing to purchase items must get prior approval.

"What we're trying to do is to get the staff thinking–as well as being caring and kind–about being fiscally accountable and conservative," said Reynalds.

The three-year-old shelter also has written its first annual budget, basing it on past expenditures and revenues. In the past it operated from month-to-month, with bills paid on a priority basis.

Because the shelter depends on donations that vary

> from month to month and because the number of people using the shelter varies, it was difficult to write a strict budget, officials said.
>
> The shelter still is seeking money to beef up its finances and to save for summer months when fewer donations come in.
>
> The $325,000 budget for 1990-91 provides money for shelter services, administration, fund raising and education. The $13,200 education budget is spent on items such as Joy Junction billboards, postage and costs of a twice-weekly radio spot updating shelter news. (*The Albuquerque Journal*, 1990. Used by permission.)

Reading that article thrilled me because it seemed that all of our hard work, diligence, and paying prompt attention to correct our faults was paying off.

However, it was the editorial in the *Albuquerque Journal* a few days later that really thrilled me. The prior one had been so caustic that this was like night and day. The editorial was headlined "Shelter Gets Businesslike."

> After three years of service to Albuquerque's unfortunates, Joy Junction has bowed to the inevitable by formulating its first-ever annual budget and putting its financial affairs under the watchful eye of a business manager.
>
> The community's well-known shelter for families had heretofore operated from month to month, with no financial planning or longer term budgeting–until the resulting financial problems threatened to sink it.
>
> "We have to show the community that what we are is what we say we are," said the Rev. Jeremy Reynalds, executive director. "We have to show integrity in the way we handle donors' money."
>
> Under the direction of business manager Frank Tercero, Joy Junction now has a system of spending controls, a formalized procedure for issuing checks and a year-round budget designed to stretch its finances over the traditionally contributions-shy summer months.
>
> Joy Junction provided temporary housing to 2,933 people

> from January through October. In its three years of existence it has become an indispensable part of Albuquerque's safety net of concern for those in need. Its new, more businesslike financial structure should enable it to build on past success and continue its caring service to the community. (*The Albuquerque Journal*, 1990. Used by permission.)

What a blessing that editorial was. And that was how we dealt with bad press. I thought it would be much better to reprint all the articles and show how the press reported the working out of our problems rather than have me say how we did it.

Good Intentions Aren't Enough

In a nutshell, we coped with bad press by acknowledging responsibility for the problems, working to solve the problems, and changing the way we did business. I believe the community forgave us for our mistakes because we did this. *Never try to blame someone else*. Everyone is sick of religious people not taking responsibility for their actions.

Now Joy Junction would have never gotten the bad press if we had realized the shelter was growing and what happens to growing organizations, whether or not they are Christian. Many organizations have a growth crisis in their third or fourth year. How they handle that crisis will determine the fate of the organization. If the crisis is handled in the right way, the organization will go on to bigger and better things. If it's handled incorrectly, or not handled at all, then the result could be the demise of the organization.

Now if I had realized what was happening with the shelter (and there were plenty of warning signs), I should have gotten a business manager before the situation became front-page press.

But my second chance came via how I reacted to the publicity that resulted from all the problems. If I had failed to make changes, then I have no doubt that the shelter would have gone under. But I changed, and the public is very forgiving of honest mistakes. And then of course, there were never any allegations of inappropriate financial conduct.

When I started the shelter, I had no idea how fast it would grow. And I initially did absolutely everything. There was no other way to do it. I did the books, paid the bills, preached the sermons, taught the evening Bible study, as well as taking over all the other seemingly endless number of chores that go along with running a shelter.

The shelter quickly began to grow, and along with that growth there was an income growth. We had a volunteer CPA, an almost volunteer bookkeeper, whom I trusted to do all the books and failed to oversee what she was doing.

Be Careful–It's Not Your Money!

My business experience was very limited, and it just didn't occur to me that a shelter with a third of a million dollars budget was in dire need of a business manager. So I kept on doing everything, but like anyone else I easily gravitated to my real interests–in marketing, PR, speaking, and so on. My real interests were definitely not in balancing the checkbook!

My big mistake was in not seeing that we had reached a growth crescendo and that, with the amount of money we were pulling in, that things just couldn't be done in the same way as they had always been done. There had to be a much clearer delineation of my responsibilities, and someone had to come in and help take some of the weight off my shoulders.

Any para-church CEO or mission executive reading these pages, please read the following very carefully. What I am going to tell you next will be very difficult for you. But it has to be done for your protection and for the good of the shelter.

Find a good business manager, one whom YOU trust implicitly, and hand over the shelter checkbook to him. It will be one of the hardest things that you'll ever do, but for your protection and the shelter's good, it has to be done.

So to summarize: You have a shelter. It's a commitment. Hang in there. God sees what you do and why you do it. You have to keep a high profile in the community, but in so doing you need to recognize that while you may not accept public funding, you are still accountable to your donor constituency as to how you spend their money.

Change

Be open to change, and be willing to let go. All things change, and as they do, they will never be the same as they once were. Don't over-romanticize the past. While it might have been good, it wasn't heaven.

Failure to recognize the need for change and the need to act accordingly will (or could) run you into problems similar to ours. Your problems might not be the same, as you may have more of a financial inclination, but the shelter will suffer in other ways.

If you do become the victim of bad or questionable press, if there is any fault on your part, own up to it, accept responsibility, and act accordingly. Even if the fault lies with members of your staff, guess what? You still get blamed, as you're the head.

I pray that the instruction contained in this chapter will help you recognize problems, and the need to act accordingly, so it doesn't make the headlines in your hometown newspaper.

Chapter Fourteen

It's Open–Are You Still Excited?

So the shelter's open, and it's been open awhile. Are you settling down to the "grind" (yes, grind!) of being the executive director of a shelter for homeless families (or the head of a Christian school, the pastor of a brand new church, etc.)?

Maybe some of you will take issue with me on calling the job a grind, so let me explain exactly what I mean by that.

Before your ministry opened, I hope God gave you a vision, a calling, or any of the other numerous names that Christians use when they believe God speaks to them or calls them to perform a particular function or task. If He did, I'm willing to bet that it's the fact of God having given you clear instructions to do what you do that has kept you going in many cases. So am I right in saying that before the ministry was opened it was all you thought or dreamed about? You saw the need out there. You recognized the lack of resources. You saw the difference that a relationship with Jesus Christ could make in the life of a troubled person, and you felt a calling to do something about it.

You just couldn't wait to get into the office in the morning. In fact, the nights were too long for you, so sometimes you stayed real late and went back really early. Then there were the nights unknown to any of the staff that you drove close to the mission (agency) and up and down the street outside just to "make sure" that everything was OK.

Your vision and calling were still very clear. They weren't only written down as your mission statement on a piece of paper, but they were burning daily in your heart. You ached for the Bible study time to come around, so you could share with the hurting women, families, and children what a difference Jesus could make in their lives.

You lived and breathed homeless families, troubled people, because you could see them after Jesus had gotten a hold of their life. You could see the difference the Lord could make. You loved the shelter and all the associated problems therewith.

There was your church's Bible study every Thursday and the home fellowship group, but somehow something always seemed to come up to prevent you from going. There seemed to be a round of constant emergencies, especially at the times you had formerly carved out for church services, Bible studies, and even your own quiet time.

Your wife reminded you of the importance of keeping a fresh, vital walk with the Lord, and while you mentally assented, you still made excuses.

"Honey, starting a ministry is just like starting a business. I'm the only one . . ."

Things continued like that for a long time, and you couldn't even remember when you last attended three or even two church services in a week. Your wife gave up asking. Outwardly, things were still the same. Inwardly, it was another matter. The Lord had blessed the ministry with great success, both financially and in the number of people He allowed to be directed to it seeking help, but . . .

And then "that day" happened! It had already been a trying month financially for the ministry, and you were stressed out "to the max."

A couple knocked at the office door just as you were in the middle of doing a dozen tasks–all legitimate and very time consuming–in the time that it should have taken to do just one.

You sighed wearily and said rather testily, "Come in."

The couple came in, and as they were relating their story

you very quickly realized it was the same story with a variation on a theme that you had heard all that week and for many months prior. After a few minutes, you said that you would "pray about their need" and politely showed them the office door.

And then it hit you! You suddenly realized that you had absolutely no intention of praying for them at all and that the whole session had been a total cop-out designed to get them out of the office as quickly as possible. You also realized that you weren't overly concerned about their eternal destiny either. *You just wanted them out of your office, and you didn't care if you never heard another homeless, drug-alcohol-related chronicle again in your life.*

You say, "Oh, that could never happen to me!"

Oh no? It sure could! The best way to guard against it is to keep your walk with the Lord strong and constantly reaffirm on a daily basis why you are running the shelter. A major reason should be that you are functioning as a tangible expression of the love of Jesus Christ to a sick and dying world.

In addition, while you are obviously supplying many physical needs, that is an offshoot of your primary purpose of seeing souls saved and come to new life in Christ Jesus.

Secondarily, you must make church and Bible study attendance a must in your life.

It never fails to amaze me that I can go many evenings without there being a crisis at the shelter, but when I go out, or try to go out, now that's another story. Take earlier this week. The contemporary Christian singer Stephen Curtis Chapman was in town for a concert. The shelter was given some complimentary tickets, and I went along as one of the chaperones for the children that we took.

The concert had just started when my "constant companion" (my digital beeper) started to vibrate. It was a message from one of my staff asking me to call him immediately. I called and was initially unable to get through. After almost ten minutes, I succeeded, took care of the crisis, and then went back into the concert.

Guess what? A few minutes later, the familiar vibration

went off again. I looked at the message, and this time it was someone from a local television station. The individual told me that she had received my fax earlier in the day asking that they consider running a story detailing the problems we had encountered with our new buildings. Could they, she asked, send a reporter down the next afternoon?

As you can imagine, by this time the concert was progressing well, without me! The whole evening served as a reminder to me that we are also battling principalities and powers and that we wage against real demonic powers, all designed to frustrate us and get our eyes off the Lord.

The interruptions could be a homeless family trying to relate their saga to you when you're totally burned out, or a TV reporter calling you when you would really like to get into a concert. Just keep your eyes on the Lord and remember that the devil doesn't bother with anyone that he's not worried about!

Chapter Fifteen

— * —

Making Time for the Press

All in a day's work! It's worth emphasizing here that I have always, and will always, take calls from the press anytime of the day or night. Press deadlines don't wait until we feel like dealing with them. Accommodate the media's schedule. Don't try and make them fit into yours. They can't and won't.

Here's one press release that got after-hours attention and made the interruptions worthwhile.

> While Democrats cheered and rejoiced Tuesday, and Republicans wept, there were homeless people looking for a place to stay.
>
> And Joy Junction was there!
>
> It was cold last night. Thank God that Joy Junction was there. If the need continues to grow at the current alarming rate, Joy Junction will soon run out of space for all the people who are looking to us for help. Women, children, families! No place to go without Joy Junction.
>
> But a shelter director's worst nightmare is beginning to unfold before his eyes! Outside my office are two beautiful buildings, almost ready for habitation by needy families. Combined, these two buildings comprise 14 rooms and eight bathrooms. Once they are completed, Joy Junction will be able to house more people in dignity.
>
> However, we face going through the winter looking at two empty buildings and having to turn away needy,

> hurting people because of an inability to generate funding to satisfy the Bernalillio County Fire Marshall's (very reasonable) requirements of installing two fire hydrants and a sprinkler system.
>
> While many Americans are basking in the warm after glow of what they feel is a new and positive direction for America, many of their fellow Americans are cold and homeless, and many more face that possibility if this project is not successfully completed in time.
>
> And will Bill Clinton's ascendancy to the presidency result in any benefits for the homeless? I seriously doubt it.
>
> There are no economic quick fixes in store for this country!

The result of that press release was a story in the afternoon Albuquerque newspaper, two stories on the local CBS affiliate, and one story on the local ABC affiliate. And that story in the afternoon paper resulted in a twenty-five thousand dollar gift allowing us to finish this project. Fifty-six more people housed—what a blessing. That article in the afternoon Albuquerque newspaper appeared on a Friday, and the next morning a man called and asked if twenty-five thousand would be a help to us. Without losing any time, I very quickly assured him it would be, so he asked if I had time to come and get it. Taking one of our board members, we made our way to this gentleman's house as quickly as we could. This was one of many ways that God has used the media to allow us to more effectively meet the needs of the homeless.

Having a flexible schedule to accommodate the needs and deadlines of the media is very important. The two stories on the CBS affiliate were filmed on a Sunday afternoon just after I came home from church. Don't (please!) tell the media that Sunday is your day off and could they come back when you're "on!" They won't, and you'll jeopardize, if not totally ruin, a great contact.

The ABC affiliate interview was filmed live outside in the freezing cold, again after my "work day" had ended. There really are potentially limitless possibilities if you're willing to work with the media.

You have to balance all this extra-curricular work with getting adequate rest and relaxation. Learn to take advantage of the quiet times, and go with the flow! Your future is very important. The Bible says that without a vision the people perish. A vision for and a sense of excitement about the future will keep you motivated. It will also give you a sense of accomplishment.

In ministry when you're dealing with so many "intangibles," it helps to break some of, or all of, your day into "bite-sized chunks." You then have something definite that you're trying to accomplish, and, having accomplished it, you can look back and be proud of what you've done.

This is really more important than it initially appears. Being able to focus on a sense of accomplishment about past efforts will help you keep going through the hard times ahead.

Chapter Sixteen

Expansion

Joy Junction has expanded slowly but surely since the shelter's inception. The need for the services offered by the shelter has grown and grown, and the overall need doesn't show any signs of decreasing. As you read the newspapers, I'm sure you've been stunned by the amount of violence in the world. Our society is having to cope with ever-increasing problems, and that includes alcoholism, drug abuse, homelessness, and AIDS.

Yes, AIDS. I've been thinking about what is going to happen to the need for shelters as the AIDS crisis gets worse and worse. Think over the following possible scenario with me.

I personally believe that very few people, if any, have any idea of what the real situation is regarding AIDS. I believe that we would see terrible riots in America if the Atlanta-based Centers for Disease Control was to reveal how many people really have AIDS. Sooner or later, that figure–the real figure–is going to catch up with us. Think of the life-insurance policies. We already have companies who are willing to reimburse 65 percent of life insurance policies to the terminally ill.

AIDS care is so expensive that even what seems initially like a tremendous amount of money can be quickly swallowed up by the astronomical price of hospital care. When all the money is gone, when hospitals can't take the terminally ill anymore, when AIDS patients are evicted from their homes because of an inability to pay the rent or the mortgage, where are they going to go?

I don't know of any other available places than shelters for the homeless run by caring, compassionate Christians. If not the only reason, that's a major reason for keeping an eye open to the possibility of expansion.

I firmly believe that we have a strong biblical mandate to share the love of Jesus Christ with the terminally ill. After all, if those who call themselves Christians won't take care of AIDS patients and the terminally ill, who will?

Just after the election of Bill Clinton as president, the following quote was in one of the Albuquerque newspapers.

> They (the Democrats) won election as advocates of change. Now high hopes meet hard reality. A Democratic Party activist was quoted as saying that Bill Clinton and Al Gore can't fix the economic situation overnight. "There's no magic wand that can undo what's been done in the last 12 years."

You see, politicians and elections and election promises come and go, but Christians and the Word of the Lord abide forever.

I think you need to regard it as an absolute certainty that there will in the foreseeable future be, not only a need, but an increasing need for the services your shelter offers (or will offer). Don't let the needs engendered by a bad economy take you unaware–be prepared.

When you think of expansion or buying your property, you should be thinking of two words: capital campaign. If you're not thinking of those words, you need to be.

A capital campaign can be a tremendous blessing to you if it's handled the right way with the right people. Otherwise, it will be a millstone hanging around your neck, the negative results of which you could feel for many years to come.

The first move you need to make when investigating the possibility of a capital campaign is to do a feasibility study. That'll tell you if a capital campaign is feasible for your organization, i.e., do you have enough support or potential support?

Your next move hinges upon the results of the feasibility study. Make sure that you have the right people handling the study. Marketing people are very expensive, but you're paying for their expertise. They have the skill to do a good job for you.

If you can get free help, maybe it's worth giving it a try, but make sure the help you get is competent and efficient. Remember that if you get free help, you really have little if any recourse if there's a problem, and your whole venture may end up getting ruined.

I would encourage you to contract out the capital campaign to paid professionals. Feasibility studies and many other aspects of marketing might look easy, but they are a skilled science. Just as the marketer wouldn't presume to do your job for you but would leave it to you as the professional, so you should leave this particular aspect of work to him or her. Marketing professionals have spent years honing their skills in an attempt to be the best at what they do. Take advantage of their skills, but don't expect to gain access to that expertise for nothing.

If the results of your feasibility study indicate that you should go ahead and launch into a capital campaign, then consult with your board and your marketing firm, then go ahead and start work.

It's very important to set a realistic goal. I would also recommend that you don't "go public" with the campaign until you have raised about half of the desired amount. Let me explain.

People like to get involved with a successful project. If you're attempting to solicit monies and involvement and you announce a goal of, say, $1 million and you're asking for money, you'll probably get asked how much you've raised so far.

When you go public, think how impressive it would be to announce that while the shelter has a goal of $1 million, you have already raised half or over half of that. Such an announcement provides incentive for people to "get on board" who might otherwise not want to do so.

And a word on setting a realistic goal: say you decide that your goal is $2 million, but you only raise one-and-a-half million dollars. Now you might have had a very successful campaign, but in the mind of the community it will always be linked with failure because you didn't raise what you said you were going to. People tend to have long memories for the wrong things. They remember failure, but sometimes block success out of their memory. Be careful!

If you would like help in choosing a consultant for your capital campaign, write to me in care of the publishers. I would be glad to help.

At the time of writing, America had just selected a new president. I don't think that Bill Clinton will particularly improve the lot of the homeless. His hands are tied by many other maybe more pressing economic needs that America now has. The private sector in general and the body of Christ in particular are the key to meeting the needs of America's homeless families. People like you are playing a major part.

Continue to seek God as to whether starting and/or running a shelter for homeless families, a drug and alcohol rehab, a crisis pregnancy center, a daytime drop-in center, or a church is what He wants you to do. If it is, then ask Him to guide you, lead you, and provide for you. Be open, receptive, and obedient, and then move and obey.

I pray that this book will play at least some part in helping your vision to minister the love of Jesus Christ to the needy—whether they be homeless or not—become a reality.

God bless you. If I can help in any further way, please do not hesitate to contact me.

More Goods Books from Huntington House

How to Homeschool (Yes, You!)

by Julia Toto

Have you considered homeschooling for your children, but you just don't know where to begin? This book is the answer to your prayer. It will cover topics, such as; what's the best curriculum for your children; where to find the right books; if certified teachers teach better than stay-at-home moms; and what to tell your mother-in-law.

ISBN 1-56384-059-6 $4.99

Battle Plan: Equipping the Church for the 90s

by Chris Stanton

Already into the nineties and it's easy to see that the institutions of American society—the family, the church, the government—will continue to look little like the same entities of all prior decades! The evidences have been discussed before. Now is the time to talk about why and what to do about it. A new battle plan is needed. The author dissects the characteristics of the enemy and the effectiveness of its attacks on the church. Then he lays out the military strategy for the spiritual warriors of the 1990s. The enemy won't know what hit him if the Church diligently readies itself for this all-important battle!

ISBN 1-56384-034-0 $7.99

You Hit Like a Girl

by Elsa Houtz & William J. Ferkile

Rape—it's the issue that dominates the headlines. Have things changed since the days when women and children were afforded respect and care by all members of society? What does self-protection mean in the 1990s in this age of higher rates of violent crime and the "progressiveness" of the women's movement? What can women do to protect themselves? What can men do to protect the women they love—or the children they'd sacrifice their very lives to shelter from harm? The authors, self-defense experts, have developed a thorough guide to self-protection that addresses the mental attitude of common sense safety and details the practical means by which women can protect themselves and their children.

ISBN 1-56384-031-6 $9.99

One Year to a College Degree

by Lynette Long & Eileen Hershberger

College: Anyone who's been through the gauntlet of higher education's administrative red tape can attest to the frustration and confusion that accompanies the process. Twenty-eight years after a failed first semester, coauthor Eileen Hershberger embarked on the admirable, albeit frightening venture, as an adult learner. One year later she earned her bachelor's degree. With Lynette Long, she reveals the secret in this thorough self-help book, complete with reference guide, work sheets, and resource lists. Most intriguing are the inside tips only professors and upper-level counselors would know.

ISBN 1-56384-001-4 $9.99

Exposing the AIDS Scandal

by Dr. Paul Cameron

Where do you turn when those who control the flow of information in this country withhold the truth? Why is the national media hiding facts from the public? Can AIDS be spread in ways we're not being told? Finally, a book that gives you a total account for the AIDS epidemic, and what steps can be taken to protect yourself. What you don't know can kill you!

ISBN 0-910311-52-8 $7.99

Loyal Opposition: A Christian Response to the Clinton Agenda

by John Eidsmoe

The night before the November 1992 elections, a well-known evangelist claims to have had a dream. In this dream, he says, God told him that Bill Clinton would be elected President, and Christians should support his Presidency. What are we to make of this? Does it follow that, because God **allowed** Clinton to be President; therefore, God **wants** Clinton to be president? Does God **want** everything that God **allows**? Is it possible for an event to occur even though that event displeases God? How do we stand firm in our opposition to the administration's proposals when those proposals contradict Biblical values? And how do we organize and work effectively for constructive action to restore our nation to basic values?

ISBN 1-56384-044-8 $8.99

A Jewish Conservative Looks at Pagan America

by Don Feder

With eloquence and insight that rival contemporary commentators and essayists of antiquity, Don Feder's pen finds his targets in the enemies of God, family, and American tradition and morality. Deftly . . . delightfully . . . the master allegorist and Titian with a typewriter brings clarity to the most complex sociological issues and invokes giggles and wry smiles from both followers and foes. Feder is Jewish to the core, and he finds in his Judaism no inconsistency with an American Judeo-Christian ethic. Questions of morality plague school administrators, district court judges, senators, congressmen, parents, and employers; they are wrestling for answers in a "changing world." Feder challenges this generation and directs inquirers to the original books of wisdom: the Torah and the Bible.

ISBN 1-56384-036-7 Trade Paper $9.99

ISBN 1-56384-037-5 Hardcover $19.99

Political Correctness: The Cloning of the American Mind

by David Thibodaux, Ph.D.

The author, a professor of literature at the University of Southwestern Louisiana, confronts head on the movement that is now being called Political Correctness. Political correctness, says Thibodaux, "is an umbrella under which advocates of civil rights, gay and lesbian rights, feminism, and environmental causes have gathered." To incur the wrath of these groups, one only has to disagree with them on political, moral, or social issues. To express traditionally Western concepts in universities today can result in not only ostracism, but even suspension. (According to a recent "McNeil-Lehrer News Hour" report, one student was suspended for discussing the reality of the moral law with an avowed homosexual. He was reinstated only after he apologized.)

ISBN 1-56384-026-X Trade Paper $9.99

The Media Hates Conservatives: How It Controls the Flow of Information

by Dale A. Berryhill

Here is clear and powerful evidence that the liberal leaning news media brazenly attempted to influence the outcome of the election between President George Bush and Candidate Bill Clinton. Through a careful analysis of television and newspaper coverage, this book confirms a consistent pattern of liberal bias (even to the point of assisting the Clinton campaign).

The major media outlets have taken sides in the culture war. Through bias, distortion, and the violation of professional standards, they have opposed the traditional values embraced by conservatives and most Americans, to the detriment of our country.

ISBN 1-56384-060-X $9.99

Kinsey, Sex and Fraud: The Indoctrination of a People

by Dr. Judith A. Reisman and Edward Eichel

Kinsey, Sex and Fraud describes the research of Alfred Kinsey which shaped Western society's beliefs and understanding of the nature of human sexuality. His unchallenged conclusions are taught at every level of education—elementary, high school and college—and quoted in textbooks as undisputed truth.

The authors clearly demonstrate that Kinsey's research involved illegal experimentations on several hundred children. The survey was carried out on a non-representative group of Americans, including disproportionately large numbers of sex offenders, prostitutes, prison inmates and exhibitionists.

ISBN 0-910311-20-X $10.99

Gays & Guns The Case against Homosexuals in the Military

by John Eidsmoe

The homosexual revolution seeks to overthrow the Laws of Nature. A Lieutenant Colonel in the United States Air Force Reserve, Dr. John Eidsmoe eloquently contends that admitting gays into the military would weaken the combat effectiveness of our armed forces. This cataclysmic step would also legitimize homosexuality, a lifestyle that most Americans know is wrong.

While echoing Cicero's assertion that "a sense of what is right is common to all mankind," Eidsmoe rationally defends his belief. There are laws that govern the universe, he reminds us. Laws that compel the earth to rotate on its axis, laws that govern the economy; and so there is also a moral law that governs man's nature. The violation of this moral law is physically, emotionally and spiritually destructive. It is destructive to both the individual and to the community of which he is a member.

ISBN Trade Paper 1-56384-043-X $7.99
ISBN Hardcover 1-56384-046-4 $14.99

Don't Touch That Dial: The Impact of the Media on Children and the Family

by *Barbara Hattemer & Robert Showers*

Men and women without any stake in the outcome of the war between the pornographers and our families have come to the qualified, professional agreement that media does have an effect on our children—an effect that is devastatingly significant. Highly respected researchers, psychologists, and sociologists join the realm of pediatricians, district attorneys, parents, teachers, pastors, and community leaders—who have diligently remained true to the fight against filthy media—in their latest comprehensive critique of the modern media establishment (i.e., film, television, print, art, curriculum).

ISBN Quality Trade Paper 1-56384-032-4 $9.99

ISBN Hardcover 1-56384-035-9 $19.99

New Gods for a New Age

by Richmond Odom

There is a new state religion in this country. The gods of this new religion are Man, Animals, and Earth. Its roots are deeply embedded in Hinduism and other Eastern religions. The author of *New Gods for a New Age* contends that this new religion has become entrenched in our public and political institutions and is being aggressively imposed on all of us.

This humanistic-evolutionary world view has carried great destruction in its path which can be seen in college classrooms where Christianity is belittled, in the courtroom where good is called evil and evil is called good, and in government where the self-interest of those who wield political power is served as opposed to the common good.

ISBN 1-56384-062-6 $9.99

I Shot an Elephant in My Pajamas—The Morrie Ryskind Story

by Morrie Ryskind with John H. M. Roberts

The Morrie Ryskind story is a classic American success story. The son of Russian Jewish immigrants, Ryskind went on to attend Columbia University and achieve legendary fame on Broadway and in Hollywood, win the Pulitzer Prize, and become a noted nationally syndicated columnist. Writing with his legendary theatrical collaborators George S. Kaufman and George and Ira Gershwin, their political satires had an enormous impact on the development of the musical comedy. In Hollywood, many classic films and four of the Marx Brothers' sublime romps also bear the signatory stamp of genius—Morrie Ryskind.

Forced by his increasingly conservative views to abandon script-writing in Hollywood, Ryskind had the satisfaction near the end of his life to welcome into his home his old friend, the newly elected President of the United States, Ronald Reagan.

In 1983, at the age of 89, Morrie Ryskind finally heeded the pleas of many friends and began work on his autobiography, working in collaboration with John H. M. Roberts. *I Shot an Elephant in My Pajamas* is the result. You will find that this too-long delayed book was well worth the wait.

ISBN 1-56384-000-6 $12.99

Deadly Deception

by Jim Shaw & Tom McKenney

For the first time the 33 degree ritual is made public! Learn of the "secrets" and "deceptions" that are practiced daily around the world. Find out why Freemasonry teaches that it is the true religion, that all other religions are only corrupted and perverted forms of Freemasonry. If you know anyone in the Masonic movement, you must read this book.

ISBN 0-910311-54-4 $8.99

When the Wicked Seize a City

by Chuck & Donna McIlhenny with Frank York

A highly publicized lawsuit . . . a house fire-bombed in the night . . . the shatter of windows smashed by politically (and wickedly) motivated vandals cuts into the night . . . All because Chuck McIlhenny voiced God's condemnation of a behavior and life-style and protested the destruction of society that results from its practice. That behavior is homosexuality, and that life-style is the gay culture. This book explores: the rise of gay power and what it will mean if Christians do not organize and prepare for the battle, and homosexual attempts to have the American Psychiatric Association remove pedophilia from the list of mental illnesses (now they want homophobia declared a disorder).

ISBN 1-56384-024-3 $9.99

Dinosaurs and the Bible

by David W. Unfred

Every reader, young and old, will be fascinated by this ever-mysterious topic—exactly what happened to the dinosaurs? Author David Unfred draws a very descriptive picture of the history and fate of the dinosaurs, using the Bible as a reference guide. Did dinosaurs really exist? Does the Bible mention dinosaurs? What happened to dinosaurs, or are there some still living, awaiting discovery?

ISBN Hardcover 0-910311-70-6 $12.99

Hidden Dangers of the Rainbow

by Constance Cumbey

The first book to uncover and expose the New Age movement, this national #1 best-seller paved the way for all other books on the subject. It has become a giant in its category. This book provides the vivid expose of the New Age movement, which the author contends is dedicated to wiping out Christianity and establishing a one world order. This movement, a vast network of occult and pagan organizations, meets the tests of prophecy concerning the Antichrist.

ISBN 0-910311-03-X $9.99

The Extermination of Christianity-A Tyranny of Consensus

by Paul Schenck with Robert L. Schenck

If you are a Christian, you might be shocked to discover that: Popular music, television, and motion pictures are consistently depicting you as a stooge, a hypocrite, a charlatan, a racist, an anti-Semite, or a con artist; you could be expelled from a public high school for giving Christian literature to a classmate; and you could be arrested and jailed for praying on school grounds. This book is a catalogue of anti-Christian propaganda—a record of persecution before it happens!

ISBN 1-56384-051-0 $9.99

Subtle Serpent: New Age in the Classroom

by Darylann Whitemarsh & Bill Reisman

There is a new morality being taught to our children in public schools. Without the consent or even awareness of parents—educators and social engineers are aggressively introducing new moral codes to our children. In most instances, these new moral codes contradict traditional values. Darylann Whitemarsh (a 1989 Teacher of the Year recipient) and Bill Reisman (educator and expert on the occult) combine their knowledge to expose the deliberate madness occurring in our public schools.

ISBN 1-56384-016-2 $9.99

New World Order: The Ancient Plan of Secret Societies

by William T. Still

For thousands of years, secret societies have cultivated an ancient plan which has powerfully influenced world events. Until now, this secret plan has remained hidden from view. This book presents new evidence that a military take-over of the U.S. was considered by some in the administration of one of our recent presidents. Although averted, the forces behind it remain in secretive positions of power.

ISBN 0-910311-64-1 $8.99

Inside the New Age Nightmare

by Randall Baer

Now, for the first time, one of the most powerful and influential leaders of the New Age movement has come out to expose the deceptions of the organizations he once led. New Age magazines and articles for many years hailed Randall Baer as their most "radically original" and "advanced" thinker . . . "light years ahead of others" says leading New Age magazine *East-West Journal.* His best-selling books on quartz crystals, self-transformation, and planetary ascension have won worldwide acclaim and been extolled by New Agers from all walks of life.

Hear, from a New Age insider, the secret plans they have spawned to take over our public, private, and political institutions. Discover the seduction of the demonic forces at work—turned from darkness to light, Randall Baer reveals the methods of the New Age movement as no one else can. Find out what you can do to stop the New Age movement from destroying our way of life.

ISBN 0-910311-58-7 $8.99

The Liberal Contradiction

by Dale A. Berryhill

Why are liberals who took part in student demonstrations in the 1960s now trying to stop Operation Rescue from using the very same tactics? Liberalism claims to advocate some definite moral positions: racism and sexism are wrong; tolerance is right; harming the environment is wrong; protecting it is right. But, contemporary liberalism is undermining its own moral foundation. It contends that its positions are morally right and the opposites are wrong, while at the same time, it denies that a moral law (right and wrong) exists. This is the **Liberal Contradiction** and it leads to many ludicrous (and laughable) inconsistencies.

ISBN 1-56384-055-3 $9.99

Trojan Horse—
How the New Age Movement Infiltrates the Church

by Samantha Smith & Brenda Scott

New Age/Occult concepts and techniques are being introduced into all major denominations. The revolution is subtle, cumulative, and deadly. Through what door has this heresy entered the church? Authors Samantha Smith and Brenda Scott attempt to demonstrate that Madeleine L'Engle has been and continues to be a major New Age source of entry into the church. Because of her radical departure from traditional Christian theology, Madeleine L'Engle's writings have sparked a wave of controversy across the nation. She has been published and promoted by numerous magazines, including Today's Christian Woman, Christianity Today and others. The deception, unfortunately, has been so successful that otherwise discerning congregations and pastors have fallen into the snare that has been laid.

ISBN 1-56384-040-5 $9.99

The Dark Side of Freemasonry

by Ed Decker

This book is probably the most significant document ever prepared on the subject of the dark side of the Masonic Lodge. In June 1993, a group of Christian researchers, teachers, and ministry leaders met in Knoxville, Tennessee, to gather together all available information on the subject of Freemasonry and its relationship to the Christian world. Ed Decker brought this explosive material back from Knoxville and here presents it as a warning to those who are unaware of the danger of the Masonic movement.

ISBN 1-56384-061-8 $9.99

Please Tell Me-Questions People Ask about Freemasonry and the Answers

by Tom C. McKenney

Since the publication of his first book, *The Deadly Deception*, Tom McKenney has appeared on over 200 talk shows, answering tough questions about Freemasonry from viewers and audiences throughout the USA and Canada. Now, in his latest book, McKenney has compiled the questions most often asked by the public concerning the cult-like nature and anti-Christian activities of the Masonic movement. McKenney tackles topics, such as; Masonry's occult roots; Death Oaths and Masonic Execution; Masonry and the Illuminati; and Masonry's opposition to Christian schools. Tom McKenney warns Christians of all denominations to extricate themselves from Masonic movements.

ISBN 1-56384-013-8 $9.99

Conservative, American & Jewish— I Wouldn't Have It Any Other Way

by Jacob Neusner

Neusner has fought on the front lines of the culture war and here writes reports about sectors of the battles. He has taken a consistent, conservative position in the academy, federal agencies in the humanities and the arts, and in the world of religion in general and Judaism in particular. Engaging, persuasive, controversial in the best sense, these essays set out to change minds and end up touching the hearts and souls of their readers.

ISBN 1-56384-048-0 $9.99

The Salt Series

To Moroni With Love

by Ed Decker

Readers are led through the deepest of the Mormon church doctrines and encouraged to honestly determine whether the words can be construed as heresy in light of the true, or as unadulterated language of the Bible. Decker reveals shocking material that has caused countless Mormons to question the church leaders and abandon Mormonism's false teachings.

ISBN 1-56384-021-9 $2.99

Exposing the AIDS Scandal

by Paul Cameron, M.D.

AIDS is 100 percent fatal all of the time. There are believed to be over 1,500,000 people in the United States carrying the AIDS virus. The ever-growing number of cases compels us to question whether there will be a civilization in twenty years.

ISBN 1-56384-023-5 $2.99

Inside the New Age Nightmare

by Randall Baer

Are your children safe from the New Age movement? This former New Age leader, one of the world's foremost experts in crystals, brings to light the darkest of the darkness that surrounds the New Age movement. The week that Randall Baer's original book was released, he met with a puzzling and untimely death—his car ran off a mountain pass. His death is still regarded as suspicious.

ISBN 1-56384-022-7 $2.99

The Question of Freemasonry

by Ed Decker

Blood oaths, blasphemy, and illegal activity—in this day and age it's hard to believe these aberrations still exist; this booklet demonstrates that the Freemasons are not simply a "goodwill," community-oriented organization.

ISBN 1-56384-020-0 $2.99

ORDER THESE HUNTINGTON HOUSE BOOKS!

Title	Price
America: Awaiting the Verdict—Mike Fuselier	4.99
America Betrayed—Marlin Maddoux	6.99
Battle Plan: Equipping the Church for the 90s—Chris Stanton	7.99
Christ Returns to the Soviets—Greg Gulley & Kim Parker	9.99
Conservative, American & Jewish—Jacob Neusner	9.99
The Dark Side of Freemasonry—Ed Decker	9.99
Deadly Deception: Freemasonry—Tom McKenney	8.99
Dinosaurs and the Bible—Dave Unfred	12.99/13.99
Don't Touch That Dial—Barbara Hattemer & Robert Showers	9.99/19.99
En Route to Global Occupation—Gary Kah	9.99
*Exposing the AIDS Scandal—Dr. Paul Cameron	7.99/2.99
The Extermination of Christianity—Paul Schenck	9.99
False Security—Jerry Parks	9.99
From Rock to Rock—Eric Barger	8.99
Gays & Guns—John Eidsmoe	7.99/14.99
Heresy Hunters—Jim Spencer	8.99
Hidden Dangers of the Rainbow—Constance Cumbey	9.99
Hitler and the New Age—Bob Rosio	9.99
How to Homeschool (Yes, You!)—Julia Toto	4.99
I Shot an Elephant in My Pajamas—Morrie Ryskind with John Roberts	12.99
*Inside the New Age Nightmare—Randall Baer	9.99/2.99
A Jewish Conservative Looks at Pagan America—Don Feder	9.99/19.99
Journey Into Darkness—Stephen Arrington	9.99
Kinsey, Sex and Fraud—Dr. Judith A. Reisman & Edward Eichel (Hard cover)	11.99
The Liberal Contradiction—Dale A. Berryhill	9.99
Loyal Opposition—John Eidsmoe	8.99
The Media Hates Conservatives—Dale A. Berryhill	9.99
New Gods for a New Age-Richmond Odom	9.99
New World Order—William T. Still	9.99
One Year to a College Degree—Lynette Long & Eileen Hershberger	9.99
Please Tell Me—Tom McKenney	9.99
Political Correctness—David Thibodaux	9.99
Prescription Death—Dr. Reed Bell & Frank York	9.99
*The Question of Freemasonry—Ed Decker	2.99
Real Men—Dr. Harold Voth	9.99
"Soft Porn" Plays Hardball—Dr. Judith A. Reisman	8.99/16.99
Subtle Serpent—Darylann Whitemarsh & Bill Reisman	9.99
*To Moroni With Love—Ed Decker	2.99
Trojan Horse—Brenda Scott & Samantha Smith	9.99
When the Wicked Seize a City—Chuck & Donna McIlhenny with Frank York	9.99
Who Will Rule the Future?—Paul McGuire	8.99
You Hit Like a Girl—Elsa Houtz & William J. Ferkile	9.99
Shipping & Handling	______
TOTAL	______

**Available in Salt Series* (marked *)

AVAILABLE AT BOOKSTORES EVERYWHERE or order direct from:

Huntington House Publishers • P.O. Box 53788 • Lafayette, LA 70505

Send check/money order. For faster service use VISA/MASTERCARD call toll-free 1-800-749-4009.

Add: Freight and handling, $3.50 for the first book ordered, and $.50 for each additional book up to 5 books.

Enclosed is $__________ including postage.

VISA/MASTERCARD#____________________ Exp. Date________

Name____________________ Phone: ( )__________

Address______________________________